JERVIS PUBLIC LIBRARY ASSN.
ROME, N.Y. 1894

PLATO ON MAN

BY THE SAME AUTHOR:

IMMORTALITY OF THE SOUL

OR

RESURRECTION OF THE INDIVIDUAL:
St. Paul's view with special reference to Plato

OBSERVATIONS ON THE CONTEMPORARY SCENE

PLATO ON MAN

A Summary and Critique of His Psychology with Special Reference to Pre-Platonic, Freudian, Behavioristic, and Humanistic Psychology

ATHENAGORAS N. ZAKOPOULOS, Ph.D.

PHILOSOPHICAL LIBRARY
New York

15 East 40th Street, New York, N. Y. 10016

Library of Congress Catalog Card No. 74-80278

SBN 8022-2153-X

Printed in the United States of America

In memory of my father, Christos; and to my mother Ourania, my sister, Lefkothea, my brothers, Athanasios, Aristotelis, Alexandros, Achilleas, and their wonderful families.

CONTENTS

INTRODUCTORY NOTE

This study investigates the psychological man embedded in Plato's writings rather than his more obvious views on man as a moral being or social or political animal. Certainly it can be argued that psychology is an incidental and peripheral theme in Plato's philosophy compared to the more central ones of ethics, politics, education and the theory of Ideas. Be that as it may, a careful and critical analysis of his psychology is, I believe, a significant undertaking. Such a critical investigation enables us to appreciate the rationality of man as well as the inner workings of the human mind and its conflicts. Further it helps us to comprehend the powerful and lasting influence Plato has exerted on those who have subsequently written on the question of man both within and outside the philosophical domain. Indeed, as the British mathematician and philosopher Alfred North Whitehead has put it with delightful exaggeration, Western philosophy proves to be nothing but a series of footnotes to Platonic thought.

The present inquiry, then, is interpretive and historical rather than speculative. It is divided into two parts with three appendices. In the first part, pre-Platonic (Homer and the pre-Socratics) views on man and his destiny are discussed. In the second and longer part, Plato's psychological theory is examined comprehensively and objectively, as it is represented in the dialogues and in the ancient, modern, and contemporary Platonic scholarship. Appendix I deals with Plato's theology. Appendices II and III compare the Platonic view of man to that of Freudian, Behavioristic and Humanistic psychology.

With reference to the chronological order and authenticity of the dialogues, I follow the generally agreed upon views of recent sholarship. J. Burnet's Oxford edition of the Greek text is used throughout. Translations are taken mainly from the standard Loeb Classical Library and from the edition of B. Jowett; on occasion translations of individual dialogues by Cornford, Hackforth, Taylor, and Lee were used.

It is my hope that this volume will prove a valuable contribution to classical, philosophical and theological investigation and to the history of psychology. As is so often the case in scholarly endeavors, in addition to important ideas expressed in the text, useful material was necessarily placed in footnotes and appendices.

ACKNOWLEDGMENTS

I should be sadly lacking in courtesy and in gratitude if I did not express my sincere thanks and indebtedness to Rev. Prof. W. Barclay and Prof. D. J. Allan, both of Glasgow University, and to Dr. D. A. Rees of Jesus College, Oxford, for kindness, for encouragement, for invaluable advice and criticism during my doctoral studies and more recently when I prepared the present study for publication. Next, I am most grateful to the following for reading the manuscript and offering helpful suggestions and valuable insights: Professors R. S. Brumbaugh, Yale University; J. E. Rexine, Colgate University; M. Marcovich and M. Naoumidis, University of Illinois; G. F. Kreyche and Rev. B. Vawter, DePaul University. My warmest thanks are also extended to Professors A. G. Nikelly and K. E. Renner, University of Illinois; and to Professors C. Chyatte and F. Heilizer, DePaul University: these psychologists were kind enough to read the sections of this volume concerning Freudian, Behavioristic, and Humanistic psychology, and to offer useful suggestions. Of course none of these men are responsible in any way for errors which may be found in this volume. I alone am responsible for those.

My sincere thanks go to the following: Revs. D. McGregor, M.A., H. MacKay, M.A., and H. Martin, M.A. for reading portions of the manuscript and discussing them with me. I am also grateful to the editors and publishers of the Philosophical Library for their advice and help and much appreciate the kind and cheerful assistance of Audrey Hodgins in the preparations of the final draft. Finally, I wish to thank Mrs. H. McGregor and Miss Meredith Smith for their skill and patience in typing the manuscript.

In closing, I would like to express my infinite gratitude to my beloved parents: my mother and late father who were my first and best teachers. Deprived themselves of higher education, they instilled in me the love (eros) of knowledge, the pursuit of education (paideia), and the thirst for truth.

PART ONE

PRE-PLATONIC BACKGROUND

Man and His Destiny

HOMER

It is extremely difficult to define the Homeric man in a modern sense, for Homer does not rely on a single word to characterize the mind or the soul;[1] indeed, "he has an unusually large psychological vocabulary."[2] However this may be, I shall deal in the following pages with three important Homeric terms: psyche, body and thymos[3] and with the Homeric concept of immortality.

A) *Psyche:*

The Homeric *psyche* means breath, breath-life, breathlike, something airy or ghostlike;[4] that is, the life-principle. Its meaning is perhaps best explained by Professor Page, who says: "*Psyche,* for which 'ghost' is a much better word than 'soul,' is not to be thought of as a spiritual essence or inmate of the body, or as the sum of its intellectual and emotional faculties. It is very like what we might call a 'ghost.' "[5] Further, this *psyche* has no connection with the living body or with any intellectual or emotional function whatsoever. Its only recorded association with the body which we find in the Homeric poems is its departure.[6] Thus, the soul may leave the body temporarily when it faints or swoons,[7] it may escape through the teeth (mouth),[8] or it may escape through "the stricken wound."[9]

B) *Body:*

Since the *psyche* holds so tenuous a relationship toward the living man, it follows that the body assumes far more importance in Homeric discussion. W. Capelle, in fact, observes that "all the activities, mental or other, of the human personality, such as feeling, thought, volition, exertion, are regarded as being possible only so long as body and soul are united; in fact they are in the strictest sense functions of the body. Menos, noos, metos, voule, thymos also are bodily faculties or powers, and although they can assert themselves only with *psyche*, at once the 'second ego' of man and the principle of his animal life remains within him, yet they are in no sense evolved from the inherent capacities of the soul which has absolutely no share in the waking activities of man."[10]

Harrison[11] notes how easily we may misinterpret Homer if we erroneously assume that his terminology neatly corresponds to modern counterparts. She goes on to observe that Homeric usage "is simply 'body,' the physical mass of which a particular man or animal is made up; and the presence or absence of life is irrelevant to the word's meaning."[12]

But which of the two component factors, psyche or body, defines the complete personality or ego? In this matter Homer is self-contradictory. In a number of passages he emphasizes soul over the body: "the wrath sent forth to Hades many valiant souls of warriors, and made themselves to be a spoil for dogs."[13] Or again, "For the whole night long hath the spirit of hapless Patroclus stood over me, weeping and wailing, and gave me charge concerning each thing and was wondrously *like his very self*."[14] Or with the soul, "until such time as I myself be hidden in Hades."[15]

The resolution, perhaps, might be expressed as follows: For Homer, neither the *psyche* alone nor the body itself is the living man or real personality or ego; rather the union or fusion of both.[16]

C) *Thymos:*

Scholars also differ regarding the *Thymos* as a third distinct entity in the living man.[17] Often *Thymos* is used in the sense of *psyche* and instead of this word.[18] Gomperz traces "a two-soul theory" in Homer and suggests that the word thymos may be taken as a second soul,[19] but E. L. Harrison challenges Gomperz's assumptions, citing his arbitrary application of the Comparative Method to Homeric studies.[20]

I find it impossible to support the contention that thymos stands for soul in the Homeric poems, in spite of the fact that scholars with etymological and linguistic skill have elaborated on this notion. The fact remains that thymos in Homer "is neither the soul nor (as in Plato) a 'part of the soul.'" Thymos, then may be defined roughly and generally as the organ of feeling,[21] as "the generator of motion or agitation while mind is the cause of ideas and images."[22]

Rohde refutes at length the Gomperz "two-soul" theory, explaining: "Again and again the thymos is clearly referred to as a mental faculty of the living body; either thinking or willing or merely feeling. . . It is the seat of the emotions. . . In the face of this, it is impossible to regard *thymos* as something independent of the body. Once indeed, H 131,[23] the thymos is spoken of instead of soul as that which goes down to Hades, but this can only be an error or an oversight."[24] Elsewhere: "In the Line H 131 we really then do have thymos instead of soul either as the result of a misunderstanding of the real meaning of the two words or merely through an oversight. But never (and this is the most essential point) do we have a case in Homer of the opposite exchange of significance, i.e. of soul used in the sense of thymos, etc. as meaning the mental power and its activity in the living and waking man."[25]

D) *Immortality:*

Now let us turn our attention to what Homer says about the soul's immortality. He writes that the soul after death leaves the body and departs to Hades,[26] that gloomy, shadowy and inaccessible land. The souls in Hades are mere images or phantoms, shades of the living man,[27] "powerless heads"[28] without wits[29] and therefore destitute of consciousness and intelligence.[30] A telling description of the Homeric souls in Hades is given by Apollodorus in his work on the Gods: Homer "assumes that the souls resemble the images appearing in mirrors and arising in water, which are made in our likeness and imitate our movements, but have no solid substance to be grasped or touched."[31]

While most souls lie unconscious and witless in Hades, a few favoured ones enjoy a happier fate. Tiresias, for example, retained his consciousness in Hades by favor of Persephone (*Od.* X 493 ff), Menelaus and Radamanthus in Elysium (*Od.* IV 561 ff), Hercules (*Od.* XI 600).[32] It is however, beyond our purposes to discuss such exceptional instances. Indeed, they are regarded by many critics, especially the Nekyia of the Odyssey, as interpolations of the later period.[33]

Even so brief a survey suggests that we will find in the Homeric poems scant consciousness of immortality after death. In fact, were we to make such an ascription, we would be very properly faulted by E. Rohde and J. Adam.[34] Indeed, life after death is so pale and empty for Homer that it is not far from non-existent.[35] "It contains no element of value that men should look forward to it."[36] The description of even so pale an existence after death suggests that Homer senses or at least does not deny the notion of immortality which was later to be more sharply defined by Plato.

1. B. Snell, *The Discovery of the Mind,* Oxford (1953) p. 8. See also E. R. Dodds, *The Greeks and the Irrational,* University of California Press (1951) pp. 15, 25, n. 95; J. Boehme, Die Seele und das Ich im Homerischen Epos, Goettingen, 1929, p. 89; H. Fränkel, Dichtung und Philosophiedes fruehen Griechentums, N.Y., 1951, p. 108; E. L. Harrison, "Notes on Homeric Psychology," The Phoenix, V. 14, 1960, 2, p. 63, n. 6.

2. J. E. Burnet, "Soul," *ERE,* XI (1920) p. 738; E. Rohde, *Psyche,* London, 1950, p. 5; T. B. L. Webster, "Language and Thought in Early Greece," Manchester Lit. and Phil. Soc. Proc. 94 (1952-53), No. 3, p. 33, calls Homer's psychological terminology "open-field terminology."

3. Other important psychological terms (or "mental organs," B. Snell, ibid., p. 12 ff; E. R. Dodds, ibid., p. 16; H. Frankel, ibid., p. 109; E. L. Harrison, ibid., p. 63, n. 7) are: "noos" or "nous," "phren," or "Phrenes," "kardia" and "kradie" and "ker" and "etor." For the various meanings of the above psychological terms, apart from the already mentioned sources, see also D. J. Furley, "The Early History of the Concept of Soul," *London Inst. of Classical Studies Bulletin,* No. 3, 1956, pp. 1-9.

4. E. Rohde, *Psyche,* p. 5; J. Burnet, "Soul," *ERE,* XI, 1920, p. 738; Idem, "The Socratic Doctrine of the Soul," *Essays and Addresses,* London, 1929, p. 142; H. G. Liddell and R. Scott, *Greek-English Lexicon,* Oxford, 1897, p. 1760; R. J. Cunliff, *A Lexicon of the Homeric Dialect,* Glasgow, 1924, p. 424.

5. D. Page, *The Homeric Odyssey,* Oxford (1955) p. 22. Similarly, S.D. F. Salmond in *The Christian Doctrine and Immortality,* Edinburgh (1895) p. 121, writes: "The *psyche* is more a physical thing than a mental; material rather than immaterial; apprehensible yet shadowy. It is the bond or principle of animal life, something more than breath but less than mind or spirit." See also E. L. Harrison. "Notes on Homeric Psychology." The Phoenix, V. 14, 1960. pp. 75-6 T. B. L. Webster "Language and Thought in Early Greece," Manchester, Lit. and Phil. Soc. Proc. 94 (1952-53), No. 3, p. 31.

6. See also E. R. Dodds, *The Greeks and the Irrational,* p. 15.

7. *Il.* V 696-7.

8. *Il.* IX 408-9

9. *Il.* XIV 518-9; *Il.* XVI 505, 856; *Il.* XXXII 362.

10. W. Cappelle, "Body," *ERE,* II, 1909, p. 769.

11. E. L. Harrison, "Notes on Homeric Psychology," The Phoenix, V. 14, 1960, 2, p. 63-64.

12. *Ibid.*, p. 64.

13. Il. I, 3-4, trans. A. T. Murray, *Homer, the Iliad,* Vol. 1, London, 1937, p. 3 in LCL; also D. B. Monro, *Homer, Iliad,* Books, I-XIII, Oxford, 1894, p. 248, who rightly translates "their bodies" and remarks, p. LXX, para. 46: "hence in Il. I 4 to distinguish the body as the actual person from the soul or life."

14. *Il.* XXIII, 104-6, trans. Ibid. Vol. II. London, 1934, p. 503.
15. *Il.* XXIII, 244, trans. A. T. Murray, *Homer, the Iliad,* Vol. II, p. 513; see also in *Il.* XI, 262-263, XIV, 456-457, XV, 251-252.
16. See also E. Rohde, *Psyche,* p. 6: "both the visible man (the body and its faculties) and the in-dwelling psyche could be described as the Man's 'self.' According to the Homeric view, human beings exist twice over; once as our outward and visible shape and again as an invisible 'image' which only gains its freedom in death. This, and nothing else, is the psyche."
17. S. G. F. Brandon, *Man and His Destiny in the Great Religions,* Manchester, 1962, p. 160, n. 5. See especially Professor R. B. Onians, *The Origin of the European Thought,* Cambridge, 1951, pp. 23-40, 44-61, 66-74, 79-83, 93-100, 103-112.
18. W. Jaeger, *The Theology of the Early Greek Philosophers,* Oxford, 1947, pp. 74-80, 82.
19. J. H. Gomperz, *Greek Thinkers,* London, 1901, Vol. 1, p. 249; and in E. Rohde's *Psyche,* pp. 50-51, n. 58.
20. The Phoenix, Vol. 14, 1960, 2, p. 69.
21. E. R. Dodds, *The Greeks and the Irrational,* p. 16.
22. B. Snell, *The Discovery of the Mind,* p. 8. Another difference between thymos and psyche is the following: When man dies the psyche survives death, being as the eidolon, the pale image, the mere shape of the former living person; while the thymos disappears, vanishes: *Iliad* 12, 386; *Iliad* 4, 524; *Iliad* 7, 131.
23. The H 131 comes from *Homer, Iliad.* E. Rohde is very unsystematic and inconsistent in his mode of quoting from ancient authorities, in spite of the fact that his translator has made an effort, as he says in his note (E. Rohde, *Psyche,* p. XV), to reduce the number of inconsistencies and to give references where possible to modern editions.
24. E. Rohde, *Psyche,* p. 50 n. 58.
25. E. Rohde, *Ibid.* p. 390 n. 2.
26. *Il.* XXII 362-3; also XX 294, XIII 415, XXIV 246; *Od.* X 560, XI 65.
27. The locus classicus is *Il.* XXII 103, 104; also see 66 ff, 99 ff; and in J. Burnet, "Soul," *ERE,* XI (1920) p. 738 n. 2.
28. *Od.* XI 29.
29. *Il.* XXIII 104.
30. *Od.* XI 476.
31. Ap. Stob. *Ecl.* 1 p. 420, quoted in J. Burnet "Soul" *ERE* Op. cit. pp. 738-9 and Idem, Socratic Doctrine of the Soul in his *Essays and Addresses,* p. 142; and E. Rohde, Psyche, pp. 7, 44, n. 6.
32. E. Zeller, *Pre-Socratic Philosophy,* I, p. 124.
33. More about it may be seen in Professor D. Page's book, *The Homeric Odyssey,* Oxford, 1955, and especially pp. 21-52, "Odysseus and the Underworld," where he points out that there was once an independent poem which was inserted to Odysseus later.
34. E. Rohde, *Psyche,* p. 9; J. Adam, *The Religious Teachers of Greece,* Edinburgh, 1923, p. 58.
35. M. P. Nilson, *A History of Greek Religion,* Oxford, 1925, p. 138.
36. A. S. P. Pattison, *The Idea of Immortality,* Oxford, 1922, p. 21.

ORPHICS

There is no real comparison between that airy ghost, the so-called Homeric psyche, and the new revolutionary idea of the Orphic Soul of divine and celestial origin. The soul for Orphics "*is a particula divinae aurae,* a particle of the pure empyrean substance or aether."[1] As Empedocles has it, it is "an exile from heaven and a wanderer."[2]

Further, we can draw a clearer picture of the Dionysiac descent (divinity) and immortality of the soul from the content of the following Orphic Plates: "I am a child of Earth and starry Heaven; but my race is of Heaven"; "I am the Son of Earth and starry Heaven"; "For I also avow that I am of your blessed race."[3] And again:

"The body of all men is subject to all-powerful death, but alive there yet remains an image of the living man; for that alone is from the gods." And finally, "It sleeps when the limbs are active, but to them that sleep in many a dream it revealeth an award of joy or sorrow drawing near."[4]

This immortal soul is sharply distinguished from the Titanic element, the body, which is regarded by the Orphics as a prison house, a grave or tomb. In their own words according to Plato and Philolaus: "Some say that the body is the tomb of the soul, as if the soul in this present life were buried; but I think it most likely that the name was given by the followers of Orpheus, with the idea that the soul is undergoing whatever penalty it has incurred and is enclosed in the body as in a sort of prison house for safe keeping."[5] Or again: "The ancient theologians and seers bear witness that for certain purposes of punishment, the soul is yoked together with the body and buried in it as in a tomb."[6]

1. J. Adam, *The Religious Teachers of Greece*, p. 99; see also S.D.F. Salmond, *Christian Doctrine of Immortality*, p. 135.

2. Emped. Frag. 115; in H. Diels ed. by W. Kranz, *Die Fragmente der Vorsokratikes* (1951) Erster Band, p. 357. See also Hippoli. Ref. VII 29. Also in F. M. Cornford, *From Religion to Philosophy*, N. Y. (1957) p. 179 n. 3.

3. J. Harrison, *Prolegomena to the Study of the Greek Religion*, N.Y. (1957) p. 575 (appendix G. Murray) 660-74; also W. K. C. Guthrie, *Orpheus and the Greeks*, London (1952) p. 173.

4. Pindar *Frag.* 131, quoted in F. M. Cornford, *Greek Religious Thought*, London (1950) p. 64.

5. *Crat.* 400 B.C., trans. F. M. Cornford, *Greek Religious Thought*, p. 74.

6. Philolaus, *Frag.* B 14; Clem. of Alex, *Miscellanies*, 117, all in DK, Vol. I, pp. 413-4.

HERACLITUS OF EPHESUS

Q. Huonder has observed that Heraclitus' doctrine of the soul bears a close relationship to his doctrine of the *Logos.*[1] It seems Huonder is not far from the truth, as *Logos* is the centre and source of all things. *Logos,* in the enigmatic, oracular and picturesque expression of Heraclitus, contains everything in himself, whatever takes place comes from him and is directed by him.

But let us examine more closely what Heraclitus himself has said about the *Logos* in relation to the human soul. In the first place, *Logos* is the ever-living fire, kindled in measure and quenched in measure.[2] This ever-living fire, the one made up of all things and from which all things issue,[3] transforms itself into sea and earth.[4] These transformations take place through strife and war,[5] through a universal and creative force, or as Heraclitus puts it, "the way up and down."[6] Within this continuous motion and change the soul also participates, becoming death, water, earth and vice-versa.[7]

Secondly, Heraclitus conceives of the *logos* as a rational entity, as wisdom, thought, and intelligence,[8] which steers the course of all things and is called Zeus or God.[9] *Logos* on the other hand, as divine law,[10] feeds the human law, prevails and suffices for all things.

Without further discussion we might well conclude from the foregoing that:

1. Heraclitus remains in the Ionian ground and expresses his ideas in a corporealistic, hylozoistic and to a great extent, pantheistic way; nonetheless, he endows his *Logos,* the ever-living fire, with intelligence and wisdom, which are to be regarded as valuable and of great importance.

2. The human soul is a portion of the ever-living fire, the divine Law, and *Logos,*[11] but it is not a separate or distinct entity or personality. Notions such as selfhood, consciousness, and immortality are completely foreign to Heraclitean theology.

3. Heraclitus mentions the life beyond when he writes: "There awaits men when they die such things as they look not for nor dream of" and again, "Souls smell in Hades."[12] But these fragments produce nothing new; indeed, they contradict the notion of "the way up and down." The soul does not survive as a permanent individual or ego after death; again this need not mean utter annihilation but rather, according to Philo, change into another element.[13]

The only sense of immortality which can be conceived of within the Heraclitean framework is one closely connected with the theory of the way up and down. J. Ithurriague has carefully analyzed this point: "We have been led to the belief that Heraclitus could not in any sense entertain the concept of individual immortality; his doctrine of eternal change precludes any such conclusion and contains no real basis on which to found belief in metempsychosis. For him, the soul, a mere spark from the universal fire, exists from all eternity. The obscure formulae in which he wraps his concepts have managed to lead certain expositors astray; they signify, however, nothing other than the series of new transformations which a man undergoes after death. In places, Heraclitus says quite explicitly, that the soul becomes water; now, since the essence of the soul is fire, such a metamorphosis can only mean extinction (literally 'death'). Consequently, the immortality of the soul can be understood only in terms of an unceasing cycle of renewals, "renouvellements," from death to life and from life to death."[14]

1. Q. Huonder, *Gott und Seele im Lichte der Griechischen philosophie,* Munchen (1954) p. 85.
2. Fr. B 30 in DK, I, p. 158.
3. Fr. 59, Fr. 22 in J. Burnet, *Early Greek Philosophy,* pp. 135, 137.
4. Fr. 21, 22 in J. Burnet, ibid, p. 135.
5. Fr. 44, fr. 62 in J. Burnet, ibid, pp. 136, 137.
6. Fr. 60 in DK, I, p. 164.
7. Fr. B 36 in DK, I, p. 159.
8. Fr. 19, 28, 91a-c, all in J. Burnet, ibid. pp. 134, 135, 139.
9. Fr. 36, 65 in J. Burnet, ibid. pp. 136, 138.
10. Fr. 91b in J. Burnet, ibid. p. 139.
11. Fr. B 115 in DK, I, p. 176; see also J. Burnet, *Greek Philosophy,* p. 59; G. Vlastos "On Heraclitus" in *American Journal of Philology,* 76 (1955) p. 438 ff; and Kirk and Raven, *The Pre-Socratic Philosophers,* pp. 206, 208, 215.
12. Fr. 27 and 99 in DK, I, p. 157; comp. also with fr. 62, 63 in E. Zeller, *Pre-Socratic Philosophy,* II, pp. 85-87; trans. J. Burnet, *Early Greek Philosophy,* p. 136, fr. 38 and 141 fr. 122. Obviously Burnet follows the arrangement of the fragments in Bywater's "exemplary" edition and not that of Diels and Kranz.
13. Philo, *De Aet. Mundi,* 21 (77.8 Cohn-Reiter on fr. 36) in W. K. Guthrie, *A History of Greek Philosophy,* I, pp. 463 n. 2 and 480 n. 1.
14. PP. *La Croyance de Platon,* pp. 120-1; see also E. Rohde, *Psyche,* pp. 368, 370, 394 n. 19; J. Adam, *The Religious Teachers of Greece,* p. 239; H. Cherniss, *Aristotle's Criticism of Pre-Socratic Philosophy,* pp. 297-8 n. 29; Kirk and Raven, *The Pre-Socratic Philosophers,* p. 210; W. Guthrie, *A History of Greek Philosophy,* pp. 479-80. While J. Burnet, *Greek Philosophy,* p. 63, admits that "there are certainly fragments that seem to assert the immortality of the individual soul; but when we examine them, we see they cannot bear this interpretation. Soul is only immortal so far as it is part of the ever-living fire which is the life of the world. Seeing that the soul of every man is in constant flux like his body, what meaning can immortality have?" Oddly enough, he checks Rohde, who "refused to admit that Heraclitus believed the soul survived death" and adds, "Strictly speaking, it is no doubt an inconsistency; but I believe with Zeller and Diels that it is one of a kind we may well admit. The first argument which Plato uses to establish the doctrine of immortality in the *Phaedo* is just the Heraclitean parallelism of life and death with sleeping and waking." It would seem that Burnet's views contradict each other.

PYTHAGORAS AND PYTHAGOREANS

Clarity concerning the soul's origin, its nature, and its immortality can not be found in the Pythagoreans because of the lack of authentic evidence and the ambiguity of the existing passages. Particularly has the famous theory of "soul-harmonia" aroused endless scholarly discussion. Nevertheless, certain generalizations may be made.

In Alexander Polyhistor's account we read that the "soul is a torn-off fragment of aither and the hot and the cold; it is not coterminous with life, and it is immortal because that from which it has been detached is immortal."[1] A further passage notes that the human soul existed before entering the human body.[2]

Aristotle also enumerates aspects of the human soul as held by the Pythagoreans, observing: "The theory held by the Pythagoreans seems to have the same purport; for some of them said that the soul is the motes in the air, others it is what moves them. They spoke of motes because they are evidently continual motion, even when there is a complete calm."[3]

The notion that the soul is either the motes in the air or that which moves them must be regarded "as a real popular belief which has already been partially elevated to a philosophical standing,"[4] and which "belong to the early and unwittingly corporealist generation which thought that units were extended in space."[5] On this H. Cherniss is most illuminating: "The 'identification' of a soul and the motes is obscure, unless it refers to an old superstition rather than a philosophical doctrine (Cf. Zeller-Nestle, op. cit. I, p. 561 n. 3) and in that case each speck of dust was probably considered to be a soul, so that Aristole's soul (psyche) implies complications which did not exist. But the 'other' Pythagoreans who identified the soul with the power that moves these motes, if they really existed, must have been very late, for their theory implies a truly immaterial soul which is simply a motor force; such a theory, since fundamentally it has nothing to do with the motes, must have been an accommodation of the earlier superstition to the more highly developed psychical theories of later times."[6]

Another Pythagorean view, again according to Aristotle is that the soul has no esoterical organic connection or "relationship" with the body; it is not what might be called the personality of the individual, visible man; "any soul may dwell in any body."[7]

But the most controversial and puzzling of all theories, which I have noted earlier and which L. Robin has termed "a subject of scandal and horror to pious Pythagoreans,"[8] remains the "soul-harmonia." According to this theory, the soul "is a kind of attunement; for attunement is a blending and composing of opposites, and the body is constituted of opposites."[9]

The first reactionary voice of opposition came from Simias, who clearly observed; "Now if the soul really is a kind of attunement, plainly when our body is unduly relaxed or tautened by sickness or some other trouble, the soul, for its divine nature, is bound forthwith to be destroyed just as much as any other attunement or adjustment in musical notes, for instance, or in a craftsman's product . . . So see what answer you can find for us to this argument, which insists that the soul, being a blending of the bodily constituent, is the first thing to perish in what is called death."[10] In other words, Simias regards the "soul-harmonia" doctrine as inconsistent with the immortality of the soul and with its transmigration. An ardent supporter of this view is Professor J. Burnet: "On the other hand nothing can be more inconsistent with earlier Pythagorean view of the soul as something that existed before the body. This doctrine, on the contrary, makes the soul a mere function of the body, and leaves no room for the belief of immortality."[11] Wilamowitz too was of the opinion that Philolaus denied the immortality of the soul and that the soul was an attunement of the bodily parts.[12]

It is beyond the scope of this discussion to review the entire matter, but it is appropriate to cite the words of the late Prof. Cornford, on the one hand, that the Pythagoreans and especially "Philolaus held that the soul is, in some sense, a harmony and that it is immortal,"[13] and, on the other hand, those of Prof. Guthrie who concluded in his remarkable *History of Greek Philosophy* as follows: "Two different notions of soul, then, existed in contemporary belief, the psyche which 'vanished like smoke' at death, and which medical writers (including no doubt some sceptical and therefore heretical Pythagoreans) rationalized into a harmonia of the physical opposites that made up the body; and the more mysterious daimon in man, immortal, suffering transmigration through many bodies, but in its pure essence divine. This too could be called *psyche,* as it was by Plato. Both survived side by side in the general current religious thought, and both also survived in the curious combination of mathematical philosophy and religious mysticism which made up Pythagoreanism."[14]

1. Diog. Laert. XIII, 24 ff. in DK, I, pp. 448-450; W. K. C. Guthrie, *A History of Greek Philosophy,* Cambridge (1962) Vol. I, p. 202. Regarding immortality of the soul comp. *Porphyrius Vit. Pythag.* 18, 19 (DK 14 8a). See also in G. S. Kirk and J. E. Raven, *The Pre-Socratic Philosophers,* Cambridge (1962) p. 223; F. M. Cornford, *From Philosophy to Religion,* p. 201 n. 1; B. Russell, *A History of Western Philosophy,* London, p. 51 n. 1.

2. Ap. Max. Tyr. 16, 2.1, 287R: qtd. in E. Rohde, *Psyche,* p. 398 p. 49.

3. Aristotle *de Anima.* A 2,404a 16; also, in G. S. Kirk and J. E. Raven, *The Pre-Socratic Philosophers,* Cambridge (1957) p. 261; DK p. 462.

4. E. Rohde, *Psyche,* p. 396 n. 40.

5. G. S. Kirk and J. E. Raven, ibid., p. 262.

6. H. Cherniss, *Aristotle's Criticism of Pre-Socratic Philosophy,* The Johns Hopkins Press, Baltimore (1935) p. 291 n. 6; W. K. C. Guthrie, *A History of Greek Philosophy,* Vol. I, Cambridge (1962) p. 307, on the other hand, notes that the first form sounds "more primitive," and the second one "a refinement on it in a spiritual direction."

7. Aristotle *de Anima* A3, 407 B 20; in G. S. Kirk and J. E. Raven, *The Pre-Socratic Philosophers,* p. 261; DK p. 462; and E. Rohde, *Psyche,* pp. 375, 396 n. 37.

8. L. Robin, *Greek Thought,* London (1928) p, 69.

9. Arist. *de Anima,* A3, 407B 20; see also in (*Pol.* VII 5 13 0 618) Diog. Laert. VIII 28, all in DK p. 462; G. S. Kirk and J. E. Raven, *The Pre-Socratic Philosophers,* p. 261; E. Zeller, *The Pre-Socratic Philosophy,* p. 476. One may also find the references in E. W. Simson, *Der Begriff der Seele, bei Plato,* Leipzig (1889) p. 15: "The soul is united to the body by means of number and harmony, indeed the soul is itself a harmony."

10. Phaedo, 86C-D, 92A-B; trans. R. Hackforth, *Plato's Phaedo,* Cambridge, 1955, p. 98.

11. *Early Greek Philosophy,* London, 1958, pp. 295-96. Idem, *Greek Philosophy,* London, 1961, pp. 92-93.

12. U. von Wilamowitz Moellendorff, *Platon,* Berlin, 1919, II, p. 90.

13. F. M. Cornford, "Mysticism and Science in Pythagorean Tradition" in *The Classical Quarterly,* Vol. XVI (1922) p. 146.

14. Cambridge, Vol. I, p. 319. Other scholars express more or less similar views on the matter, such as: F. M. Cornford, "Mystery Religions and Pre-Socratic Philosophy" in the *Cambridge Ancient History,* IV, (1926) pp. 548-9, and his *From Religion to Philosophy,* p. 213; also E. Rohde, *Psyche,* pp. 377, 400, ns. 52, 54, 55; E. Zeller, *Pre-Socratic Philosophy,* pp. 476-78; H. Cherniss, *Aristotle's Criticism of Pre-Socratic Philosophy,* p. 323; G. S. Kirk and J. E. Raven, *The Pre-Socratic Philosophers,* p. 262.

EMPEDOCLES OF ACRAGAS

Empedocles from the first holds two widely different and incompatible views regarding the nature and immortality of the soul. He observes that the physical basis of consciousness is in the blood,[1] which blood again arises from four elements.[2] Here Empedocles expresses himself in a purely materialistic way, as a "thorough materialist"[3] and leaves no room for immortality. On the other hand, in the *Purifications*, and particularly in the *Fr. 115*, he expressly states that he is calling the soul daemon, a fugitive and a wanderer from the gods.[4]

There is an apparent contradiction between these views but it is, perhaps, not an irreconcilable one. The resolution, I think, can be found in the fact that Empedocles tried to reconcile the cosmological-physical theories of his predecessors Anaximander and Parmenides, to mention only two, with their theological conclusions, a goal he was unable to achieve. As a result, Empedocles himself seems to speak with two different voices.

E. Rohde,[5] F. M. Cornford,[6] G. S. Kirk and J. E. Raven[7] attempted harmonisation. They believed themselves to have effected this quite successfully and convincingly. E. Zeller,[8] J. Burnet,[9] and J. Adam,[10] however took exactly the opposite view and reached the incontestable conclusion that the cosmologico-religious teachings of Empedocles are not only contradictory but irreconcilable.

1. Fr. 105 in DK, I, p. 350, Porphyryat Stob. Anth. I, 49, 53; and in G. S. Kirk and J. E. Raven, *The Pre-Socratic Philosophers,* pp. 344, 357.

2. Fr. 98 in DK, I, p. 346; comp. also with fr. 109, DK, ibid. p. 351; Arist. *Metaph.,* B4, 1000b; and in G. S. Kirk and J. E. Raven, ibid. pp. 335, 343 and 357. See also Aristotle, *de Anima,* A4, 408 a, 13.

3. W. Guthrie, *A History of Greek Philosophy,* I, p. 318.

4. Fr. 115; see also Hippolytus Ref. VII, 29; Plut. *de exilio* 17 607C; in G. S. Kirk and J. E. Raven, ibid., pp. 352-356.

5. *Psyche,* pp. 382-3.

6. *From Religion to Philosophy,* pp. 224-42.

7. *The Pre-Socratic Philosophers,* pp. 359-60.

8. *Pre-Socratic Philosophy,* II, pp. 176-7.

9. *Early Greek Philosophy,* p. 250.

10. *The Religious Teachers of Greece,* p. 253.

ANAXAGORAS OF KLAZOMENAI

Despite the scholarly disagreement that Anaxagoras has caused[1] the fact remains that he introduced a concept of great importance and significance to Greek philosophy – the principle Mind (*Nous*).

Anaxagoras regards the Nous as something material, corporeal, and occupying space,[2] but these are not his last words. He further characterizes Nous as "infinite and self-ruled"; it "is mixed with nothing but is all alone by itself . . . it has all knowledge about everything and the greatest power; and mind controls all things, both the greater and the smaller, that have life. . . . Mind arranged them all."[3]

Anaxagoras, then, seems to indicate that he conceived of Nous as an immanent, transcendent, spiritual, omnipotent and intelligent Deity or God.[4] Unfortunately he did not go on to elaborate this idea leaving the task for posterity. Although Anaxagoras introduced something of immense value, that is, a spiritual and intellectual principle, "he fails to understand fully the essential difference between that principle and the matter which it forms or sets in motion."[5]

It is almost impossible to attempt a clear account of the individual soul, selfhood, consciousness, immortality and self-existence in Anaxagoras, as he "n'est pas parvenu a la conception d'une âme individuelle, vivant d'une vie eternelle."[6] Indeed as Aristotle says of Anaxagoras, he does not speak clearly about Mind and soul,[7] but seems to regard them as different aspects of the same nature. On the contrary, Plato suggests that Anaxagoras uses both terms as identical and interchangeable.[8]

Rohde's remarks, perhaps, can serve as a meaningful synopsis of the Anaxagoras position: "Anaxagoras could not speak of the continued existence of individual, self-existent 'souls' after the dissolution of the material concretions in which moving and animating 'soul-force' had once lived. . . . For him the individual, the personality conscious of itself and of the outer world, can be nothing but a manifestation of the universal, whether the later is regarded as fixed and at rest, or as a living process that untiringly develops itself, recruits itself, and reconstructs itself in ever renewed creations. The only permanent, unchanging reality is the universal, the essential and fundamentally real nature which appears in all individual things, speaks out of their mouth, and in reality, only works and lives in them. The individual human soul has its identity with the universal that represents itself in it. The individual forms of 'appearance' having no independence of their own, cannot permanently abide."[9]

Finally, then, for Anaxagoras soul is a moving force[10] and has two forms, the moving and the knowing,[11] and the particular consciousness ceases to exist when the soul leaves the body.[12]

1. G. S. Kirk and J. E. Raven, *The Pre-Socratic Philosophers,* p. 367; also J. E. Raven, "The Basis of Anaxagoras' Cosmology," *Classical Quarterly,* IV (1954) p. 123; G. Vlastos, "The Physical Theory of Anaxagoras," *Philosophical Review,* 59 (1950) p. 31 ff.

2. Fr. 12 in DK, II (1952) pp. 37-39.

3. Fr. 12 in DK, ibid., comp. *Cratyl.* 413C; Aristotle *de Anima,* A2, 405 a 15, *Phys.* 5 256 b 24 and in DK, ibid. p. 20; trans. G. S. Kirk and J. E. Raven, *Pre-Socratic Philosophers,* pp. 372-3.

4. E. Zeller, *Pre-Socratic Philosophy,* Vol. II, p. 349; and J. Adam, *The Religious Teachers of Greece,* p. 263, do not find it difficult to identify Nous with God, although there is no mention at all of the word God or Gods in Anaxagoras' fragments. Later writers maintain the view: Aet 1, 7, 5 (D 299); 7, 15 (D 302) Vgl. Eur. fr. 1018. Tro ad 884 (64.2); Iambl. Protr. 8 Philed de piet. C.4 ap. 66 G (D 532). Vgl. (B12) Cic. de nat. d. I, 11, 26 (D 532) . . . qua sentire possit, fugere intellegentiae nostrae vim et rationem videtur"; Cic. Acad. Pr. II 37, 118 (D 119): "A materiam infinitam sed ex ea particulas similes inteadductas: eas primum confusas postea in ordinem adductas mente divina" qtd. in D. K. pp. 19-20; Comp. also Sext Math. IX, 6: Stob. Ecl. 1, 56; The Mist. Orat. XXVI, 317C in E. Zeller, *Pre-Socratic Philosophy,* p. 349 p. 1.

5. F. Copleston, *A History of Philosophy,* London, (1961), Vol. I, p. 70. For more on this point see J. E. Raven, "The Basis of Anaxagoras' Cosmology," *Classical Quarterly* (1954) Vol. IV, p. 134; G. S. Kirk and J. E. Raven, *The Pre-Socratic Philosophers,* p. 374; J. Adam, *The Religious Teachers of Greece,* pp. 261-264; E. Zeller, *Pre-Socratic Philosophy,* II, pp. 346-349; R. K. Gaye, *The Platonic Conception of Immortality,* p. 13; F. M. Cornford, *From Religion to Philosophy,* p. 154; W. Jaeger, *The Theology of the Early Greek Philosophy,* pp. 160-162; P. Leon, "The Homoiomeries of Anaxagoras," *Classical Quarterly,* XXI (1927 pp. 133-141; J. Burnet, *Early Greek Philosophy,* p. 268, and *Greek Philosophy,* pp. 79-80, holds the opposite view.

6. J. Ithurriague, *La Croyance de Platon,* p. 123.

7. *De Anima,* A2, 404 b. 1; and in DK, p. 29; E. Zeller, *Pre-Socratic Philosophy, II,* p. 364 n. 5, 6, p. 347 n. 2; E. Rohde, *Psyche,* n. 410, n. 115. See also Cherniss, *Aristotle's Criticism of Pre-Socratic Philosophy,* pp. 291-2 and 295-6.

8. *De Anima,* 405 a 13; *Crat.* 400 A. also in E. Zeller, *Pre-Socratic Philosophy,* II, p. 345 n. 1; E. Rohde, *Psyche,* p. 410 n. 115.

9. E. Rohde, *Psyche,* p. 388; see also J. Adam, *The Religious Teachers of Greece,* p. 264.

10. Aristotle, *De Anima,* A 2, 404 a 25; also in DK p. 29; E. Zeller, *Pre-Socratic Philosophy,* II, p. 364.

11. Psell. d. omnif. doctr. 15 in DK I, p. 29; and in K. Freeman, *Companion to the Pre-Socratic Philosophers,* A 101. a, Oxford (1946) p. 274 n.g.

12. A 103, K. Freeman, ibid. p. 274, n. i.; Aat V 252 (D. 437) in DK p. 30.

SOCRATES

Professor J. Burnet argues that Socrates for the first time introduces the notion of the human soul, of the true self,[1] with what he openly said to his fellow citizens of Athens about the soul's care and its perfection: "os tes psyches opos os ariste estai."[2]

At any rate, this asssertion does not prevent us from noting that Socrates was more concerned with the moral aspect of the soul and its perfection than with the rational and philosophical exposition of the doctrine of the soul. This great achievement was to fall to his disciple, Plato. E. W. Simson confirms this point of view: "As we consider now the psychology of Socrates, we shall find it comprehensible by his forthcoming interest in ethics that there is with him no developed doctrine concerning the nature of the soul."[3] Concerning the destiny of the soul in the life after death Socrates says: "For the state of death is one of two things; either it is virtually nothingness, so that the dead has no consciousness of anything, or it is, as people say, a change and migration of the soul from this to another place."[4] As his words stand, they express uncertainty, and caution. However, I would not hold that Socrates professes a nihilist or even agnostic view. Rather his views about the perfection of our souls[5] combine to form a basis for the assumption that Socrates was a firm believer in the hereafter. Witness the following: "Moreover, the soul of man, which more than all else that is human, partakes of the divine, reigns manifestly within us, and yet is itself unseen."[6] ". . . no evil can come to a good man either in life or after death, and God does not neglect him."[7] "I go to die, and you to live; but which of us goes to the better lot is known to none but God."[8] ". . . and so why should I not be justly accounted blessed and enjoy an immortality of fame?"[9] In summary then, Socrates "for his part, accepted one of the alternatives as his personal belief; and this alternative is not the Homeric idea of a shadowy existence in an unsubstantial Hades, nor the utter annihilation in death, but a real life, in blessedness, under the protection of the gods."[10]

1. "The Socratic Doctrine of the Soul," *Essays and Address,* London (1929) pp. 126-62, and more particularly for our case, pp. 157-61; Idem, *Early Greek Philosophy,* p. 84; Idem, "Soul," *ERE,* Vol. XI, pp. 671 and 741; his article "Philosophy" in *The Legacy of Greece* (ed. by Sir. R. Livingstone) Oxford (1957) p. 76; also in A. M. Armstrong, *An Introduction to Ancient Philosophy,* London (1959) p. 29; V. De Magalhaes-Vilhena, *La Probleme de Socrate,* Paris (1952) pp. 51, 52 n. 1.

2. *Apol.* 29E, 30A; also Xen. *Mem.* 12.

3. *Der begriff der Seele bei Plato* (1889) pp. 20, 21; also in A. E. Taylor, *Socrates,* Edinburgh (1933) p. 139: "The Socratic doctrine, we must note, is neither psychology, in our sense of the word, nor psychophysics. It tells us nothing on the question of what the soul is, except that it is in us, whatever it is in virtue."

4. Plato *Apol.* 40C 6-11, trans. H. N. Fowler, *Plato, Apology,* London, (1938) p. 141, in LCL; ibid; 29A.

5. Plato *Apol.* 29E, 30A. B.

6. Xen. *Mem.* IV, 3, 14. cf 4, *Cyrop.* VIII, 7, 9, trans. E. C. Merchant, Xenophon, *Memorabilia and Oeconomicus,* London, (MCMXXIII) (1923), p. 307 in LCL.

7. *Apol.* 41D; trans. H. N. Fowler, Op. cit. p. 145 in LCL.

8. *Apol.* 42A; trans. ibid.

9. Trans. W. Miller, *Xenophon Cyropaedia,* London, (MCMXIV) (1914) Vol. II, p. 427 in LCL.

10. E. Ehnmark, "Socrates and the immortality of the soul" in *Eranos,* Vol. XLIV (44) (1946) p. 122. Other interesting points in pp. 108, 116, 117, 119, 120, 121, 122. Also E. A. Taylor, *Plato* (*The Man and his Work*), London (1960) p. 138, n. 2. "The caution should not be understood to mean that Socrates doubts the fact of immortality. His firm belief in that is the assumption of the Phaedo and is really presupposed by Apolog. 40C-41C." Also some scholars hold moderate views: E. Zeller, *Socrates and the Socratic School,* London (1868) pp. 147-9, ns. 1, 3, 4, 5; B. Jowett, *The Works of Plato,* Vol. 3, N.Y. (Apol.) p. 99; J. J. Forbes, *Socrates,* Edinburgh (1905), pp. 232-37; R. K. Gaye, The *Platonic Conception of Immortality,* pp. 14-5; B. Russell, *History of Western Philosophy,* p. 109.

CONCLUSION

From what has been said so far, we may surmise that there will be a difference between Plato's teachings and those of his predecessors. In point of fact, most of his forerunners did not consider the nature of the soul as a separate issue, but dealt with it in connection with the universe or in a mythical and quite incomplete way.[1]

Plato was cognizant of his precursors and referred to their teachings, but he, as we shall see, approaches the psychologico-eschatological problem and metaphysics in general in a different manner. He begins by developing a theory of the soul and its life after death philosophically. He examines it in dialogue form and searches for every possible aspect in a dialectical and imaginative fashion. His predecessors, as we have seen, expressed themselves obscurely and relied on vague myths and popular beliefs, without attempting logical explanation. Plato goes on to use myths in a more logical and dialectical way.[2] He often succeeds in his challenging task, but even when he fails he has at least stated the logical questions for future speculative elaboration.

1. For moderate views on Orphico-Pythagoric influence on Plato, avoiding of course the extreme and exaggerated view of V. D. Macchioro *From Orpheus to Paul,* London, 1930, p. 176, that: "Plato's philosophy appears to be purified and enlarged Orphism" see the following scholars: H. C. Moore, *Pagan Ideas of Immortality during the Early Roman Empire,* Cambringe, 1918, pp. 14-15, 62; H. E. Smyth, *Conceptions of Immortality,* pp. 274-275, 282-283; W. K. Guthrie, Orpheus and Greek Religion, pp. 242-244; J. Adam, *The Religious Teachers of Greece,* pp. 113-114; J. Ithurriague. *La Croyance de Platon,* pp. 148-149.

Their views might be summarized as follows: Plato gave to the Orphico-Pythagoric notions about soul and its immortality, a reasoned and philosophic basis.

2. The difference which Cicero discerns between the Pythagorean and the Platonic treatment of the question seems applicable here. He writes: "They scarce ever gave any reason for their opinion, but what could be explained by numbers and characters. It is reported of Plato, that he came into Italy, to acquaint himself with the Pythagoreans; and that when there, he learned from them all the tenets of Pythagoras, concerning the immortality of the soul, but he brought reasons in support of it." Cic. Tusc. Disp., I, XVII. Trans. by W. H. Main, London, 1824, p. 23. See also R. K. Gaye, *The Platonic Conception of Immortality and its Connexion with the Theory of Ideas,* London, 1904, p. 16, n. 1. He quotes the passage in Latin.

Part Two

PLATO ON MAN

Preliminary Remarks

WHAT IS MAN?

Plato, commenting upon the etymology of the name man (anthropos) in *Cratylus,* his work on the philosophy of language, points out the essential difference between man and animals. Man, he observes, is an erect, walking animal, but he alone among all animals is a rational animal with the ability to examine, to reflect, to reason, and to form mental abstractions. Plato's description of man as a rational being, fundamental and extremely important as it is, is not his last word on the issue under discussion. Man's rationality is only one aspect of his being, and so this description remains partial and incomplete. The true, the complete definition of man, according to Plato, is as follows: man consists of two clearly distinct entities – soul and body.[2] It must be noted that this union of soul and body, as we shall discuss at greater length later, is an accidental and a temporary one. The body is mortal, earthly and transient, but the soul is an immaterial, immortal and permanent entity.[3] Implicit in this definition are two assumptions: firstly, that the soul occupies, possesses and uses the body for its biological functions; secondly, that the soul enjoys the more prominent position in this relationship.

In addition, we find in the *Alcibiades I,* of disputed authorship, the view that man is neither the body alone, nor the body and soul together, but the immortal soul itself.[4] Plato quite clearly declares in the *Laws* that man's true self resides in the divine and immortal part, that the real self of each of us is the immortal soul.[5]

With reference to the first view – that man is soul itself – I maintain that *Alcibiades I* is a spurious work which does not represent the true platonic view but rather embodies that of the religious thinkers, mystics and early members of the Academy.

With respect to the declaration in *Laws*, that man's true self is his soul, it must be noted that Plato here and in other dialogues identifies soul or mind with what contemporary philosophers and psychologists call self, ego, I, but not with what has come to be termed personality.

It must be remembered that these relatively synonymous terms (self, ego, I) are but specific parts of the human being and refer to man's consciousness, awareness and rationality, while the word man, generally speaking, corresponds to the wholeness, the totality of man. The term man incorporates the psychological, physiological and emotional aspects cf the human being, of the personality, which Freud and Jung, by the way, identify only with the psyche or mind. This subtle distinction between conscious awarness (self, ego, I) and the concept of man in his entirety can be interpreted to fit admirably the platonic case.

We maintain, then, that Plato conceives of man individually as a composite of soul and body. However, as we shall see later, he emphasizes the value and worth of the human soul in his dialogues, depreciating the body as a contemptible tool or instrument, but not ignoring it altogether.

Since we have accepted that man, for Plato, is made up of soul and body, we must turn our attention to the nature and the relationship of these separate components. It is not enough merely to set out the various references to the soul as they occur in the dialogues, since Plato's theory of the soul and its relationship with body is not rigidly uniform and occasionally is even contradictory, and we propose to treat this subject under the following headings:

A general definition of the psyche (soul).
The origin of the soul: generated or ungenerated?
The division of the soul.
Soul-body: their relationship.
The immortality of the soul.
An assessment-conclusion.

1. 399 C1-7; see also Protagoras 322 A3-10; Menexenus 237 D5-9; Epictitus Diatribe II, 9. 1-14; it is interesting to note that a number of contemporary biologists, though they adhere to the view that man in many respects is anatomically and physiologically similar to the animals, discover other characteristics which set him apart from all other animals. In point of fact, these biologists maintain that there is a vast and "unbridgeable" difference between man and animals.

The following two quotations illustrate better the point.

The biologist H. Curtis, *Biology,* Worth Publ. Co., 1968, p. 807, writes: "We know that man differs from the animals and all other organisms, however, in his power to reason and plan, to invent and manipulate, to exercise foresight, and to communicate his ideas and beliefs to his fellow man. . . . He also differs from other animals, we hope, in qualities of judgment, restraint, wisdom, tolerance, compassion, and ethical commitment, and also in his sense of wonder and beauty." Prof. W. H. Thorpe, a leading British ethologist, in his fascinating book *Learning and Instinct in Animals,* London, Methuen, 1956, p. 417, clearly distinguishes between man and animals, stressing man's unique mental, aesthetic, and religious qualities. He writes: "To assume that studies of animal behavior imply any decrease in the stature of man would be a view of the utmost naivete. . . . Man displays emergent qualities far transcending those of the highest animal. The existence of his high powers of abstract reasoning and his faith, of his religious awareness and spiritual life, his appreciation of moral and aesthetic values, his self conscious discipline of the will to achieve beauty, goodness and truth; as well as all the other manifestations of his genius that have already emerged, not only confirm this, but suggest that there are also in him vast further potentialities yet to be realized." See also in his other book *The Swarthmore Lecture: Quakers and Humanists,* London, 1968, p. 48. Similar views are also expressed in the following works: F. C. Jean, E. C. Harrah and F. L. Herman, *Man and His Biological World,* revised edition, Ginn, Boston, 1962, pp. 480-483; R. B. Platt, G. K. Reid, *Bioscience,* Reinhold Book Co., N. Y., 1967, p. 494; M. Bates, *Man in Nature,* in *Foundations of Modern Biology* series, Prentice-Hall Inc., 1964, pp. 1-11; T. Dobzhansky, *The Biology of Ultimate Concern,* A Meridian Book World Pbl., N.Y., 1971, pp. 63-80; Th. Dobzhansky, *Mankind Evolving: The Evolution of the Human Species,* New Haven, Yale Univ. Press, 1966, p. 203; G. G. Simpton, *Biology and Man,* Harcourt, Brace and World Inc., N.Y., 1969, pp. 82-92; P. Alsberg, *In Quest of Man: a biological approach to the problem of man's place in nature,* Pergamon Press, Oxford, 1970, p. 100-110; Jean-Claude Fillous, *The Psychology of Animals,* trans. by J. J. Walling, Walker and Co., N.Y., 1963, pp. 122-123 and pp. 134-138; Bierens de Haan, *Animal Psychology,* Hutchinson, London, 1946, pp. 145-147.

The British zoologist Desmond Morris, *The Naked Ape,* London, 1967, argues that man is "not only an animal but an ape," "certainly an ape." J. Lewis and B. Towers, *Naked Ape or Homo Sapiens?,* dismiss Morris' thesis in a scientific and forceful way. In their fascinating book they also criticize Freud's Lorenz's, Ardrey's, and Morris' views on aggression. For more on aggression see E. Fromm, *The Anatomy of Human Destructiveness,* Holt, Rinehart and Winston N.Y. 1973; P. W. Macky, *Violence: right or wrong?* Word Books, Waco, Texas, 1973.

2. *Phaedrus* 246C5; see also *Rep.* 462CD; *Timaeus* 34BC; 35A-B; and especially 41D4-E1; 42A-E1-4; 69B-D1, and 09A1-9; *Meno* 86AB; *Statesman* 309C1-3; *Phaedo* 76C; 79 *Epinomis* 98-A7-10.

3. *Phaedo* 80D; *Timaeus* 34C; *Laws* 892A, 967D.

4. *Alcib,* I 129E9-139A-C. *Olympiodorus commentary on the first Alcibiades of Plato* (Ed. by L. G. Westerink), Amsterdam (1956) pp. 1-15, 127-133, 202. See also apocrypha Axiochus 365.

5. *Laws* XII, 959A8, B1-5. Comp. Eth. Nic. 1168B34-35, 1777B30, 1178A1-2; also in F. M. Cornford, "The Division of the Soul," *The Hibbert Journal,* XXVIII, (1929-30) p. 209, n. 1; J. Burnet, *The Ethics of Aristotle,* London, 1900, p. 423 on 116B35, comments " . . . we are not entitled to say that this is Aristotle's own view, but it certainly was Plato's"; P. Shorey, *What Plato Said,* Chicago, 1933, p. 654 n. on *Alcib.* I. 130C3.

A GENERAL DEFINITION OF THE PSYCHE (SOUL)[1]

This definition, as the heading indicates, will be broad, and what is said here and in the next chapter ("The Origin of the Soul") applies to the cosmic as well as to the human soul.

In the first place, the main characteristic of the soul, its essence, is self-motion.[2] Further, soul is not only the self mover but the source and first principle of motion for all other things that are moved,[3] the source and origin of the life.[4] In other words, it could be said that soul is not only the source of life, the cause of it,[5] but the life itself; soul and life are one and the same thing.[6]

Furthermore, Plato notes that the soul is related to the eternal forms[7] and that it is immortal,[8] without birth, ungenerated.[9] Finally, soul is the seat of reason and intelligence[10] and of individual freedom and responsibility.[11]

1. For additional meanings of the concept of soul see in Archer-Hind, R. D., "On Some Difficulties in the Platonic Psychology," *Journal of Philology,* 10, 1882, pp. 120-131; and more particularly in Professor T. M. Robinson's extremely interesting book *Plato's Psychology,* Toronto, 1970, pp. 4-50; 116-117; 146-163.

2. *Phaedrus* 245E2-4; *Laws* 896A1-3; cf. also with Aristotle, *de Anima,* A 2 403B20-28.

3. *Phaedrus,* 245C6-9; *Laws* 895B2-4; *Laws* 896A7-9.

4. *Phaedrus* 245C7-10.

5. *Cratyl.* 399D11-12 and E1-2.

6. *Rep.* 353D7-9.

7. *Phaedo* 80B1-3; ibid; 78B8-12; ibid. 79D1-4.

8. *Phaedo* 80B1, 105E6, 106E9; *Phaedrus* 245C5; *ibid.* 246A1; *Republic,* 608D3; *Republic* 611B9.

9. *Phaedrus* 245C-246A; especially 246A1-2.

10. *Timaeus* 30B3; *Phil.* 30C8-10; *Soph.* 249A1-8; *Laws* 897B.

11. *Timaeus* 87B7-90D; *Rep.* 617E4-5.

THE ORIGIN OF THE SOUL: GENERATED OR UNGENERATED?

The creation of the soul is described in the *Timaeus* in a somewhat detailed and highly figurative manner. This is not the place to discuss at length the creation of the soul, suffice it to say this:

The Demiurge, the divine craftsman who made the cosmos and the gods, created both the world-soul and the immortal part of the human soul out of the same ingredients (the intermediate kinds of existence, sameness and difference)[1] in much the same way. The created gods made the human body and the mortal part of the human soul.[2]

Although the composition and structure of the immortal element of the human soul are identical to those of the world-soul, the human soul is a less pure blend of intermediate existence, sameness and difference.[3]

Besides this passage in the *Timaeus*, Plato, charging everyone as ignorant and knowing nothing of the origin,[4] repeatedly states in the *Laws* that soul has been produced first, came first, is the first born of all things and prior to body.[5]

The task of interpreting the soul's origin would be less complicated had Plato himself not taken a diametrically opposite view in the *Phaedrus,* observing that the soul is absolutely without beginning, uncreated and ungenerated.[6] This apparent contradiction between passages has proved disquieting to all Platonic scholars, both ancient and modern, forcing them to attempt reconciliations.[7]

With regard to Timaeus' theory of the creation of the human soul, Plato himself warns us to look upon his account of the creation, and consequently of the soul's composition as well, as a mere myth, a probable tale.[8]

The late Prof. R. Hackforth, despite Plato's warning, refers to 34C4 and seems to suggest that in *Timaeus* Plato kept in mind a soul uncreated and prior to the body.

Nevertheless, the greatest difficulty lies between the *Laws*, where Plato categorically declares soul as (892C4) first born, (896C1-2) prior to body (967D67) and "oldest of all things that partake of generation" (trans. R. G. Bury, *Plato, Laws*, II, p. 563 in LCL) and the *Phaedrus* (245C6-246A2) where Plato declares soul to be uncreated, ungenerated.

Because of the apparent conflict between the two dialogues, Plato's commentators have continued to offer solutions to this obvious antithesis.

I shall begin with Prof. Cherniss' effort at reconciliation. Cherniss defends his case as follows: "The scope of the argument in the *Laws* is determined by the thesis which it is meant to refute, namely that fire, water, earth and air are *prota* and that soul is *ek touton hysteron* (891C). To refute them he need say nothing as to whether soul is absolutely without beginning, but has only to prove that it is *presbyteran somatos*. . . . In other words, Plato does not explicitly draw the conclusion here that the soul is absolutely without beginning simply because that point is superfluous to his present argument and like a skilled debater, he confines himself both in assumption and proof to the minimum necessary for establishing his case."[9] He goes on to say that "there are clear indications in the course of the argument that he has not abandoned the position of the *Phaedrus*. In 894E-895B, he argues first that moving things necessarily imply self-motion, as the ultimate principle of their motion, and secondly that if all things should be assumed at rest, a first motion would have to be self-motion, for since there is no change in the things at rest, change induced by something other than self-motion (i.e. by a moved mover) could not be prior to this. In this passage, which is simply an expansion of *Phaedrus* 245D7-E2, the first part implies that "generated self-motion" is a contradiction in terms, and the second that, if soul, as motion, were "generated," not it but its generator would be self-motion and the *arche kineseos pason*. . . That soul is called *prote genesis* does not at all imply that it ever did not exist or was ever "generated" in the sense of being "now" after not having been "before." The soul is, of course, a "process," though not a physical process, being intermediate between the ideas and the physical universe; it too is dependent upon the real being of the ideas, but the very fact that it is called *prote genesis* of all things that are or have been or will be and of all their contraries (*Laws* 896A, 899C6-7) shows that Plato did not here envisage any "production" or "creation" of it."[10]

The late Prof. Hackforth also attempted two different explanations of the "puzzling" passages in the *Laws*.

In an earlier article, he suggests that the words "*osa gones metelefen*" (*Laws* 967D) mean "no more than genesis eldest of all things that are generated" and that "soul then is a genesis or gegonos" or "participates in birth."[11] This gegonos does not imply any creation in time and is simply a derivative existent depending on something more ultimate. Later, he held that Plato repeats and expands in the *Laws* the theory of the self-moving soul, and as it is quite natural, everyone would have expected him to reaffirm its ungenerated nature. Unfortunately, Plato refrains from doing so and instead tries "to confute the atheistic materialists who make body prior in origin to soul, he adopts their temporal category and confines himself to demonstrating the reverse priority."[12] When Rankin takes up the point, he argues that it is apparent from the *Timeaus* (37D)—and this accords with Hackforth's opinion—that Plato recognized an inadequacy in the use of language when ordinary concepts of time were employed to express cosmological ideas. The time divisions of the "temporal" world are seen as irrelevant to the "extra-temporal." As the "temporal" world is a created thing, so *also* is its character of temporality, a flickering shadow of the enduring substance of eternity. In this context, only the present tense can have any force, and *past* and *future* alike are meaningless. This is not to say that Plato never uses the "irrelevant" tenses in writing of the timeless cosmos. He acknowledges that men were conditioned to thinking in such terms and regarded it as a work of supererogation to avoid tensed language completely. This "conditioning" was expressed in the idea that *man* and *time* were, so to speak, twins – an idea inherent in much Greek writing – and found particularly in the *Laws* (721C). Time, in this system, exists by the side of man, paralleling his age at each juncture – young when he is young, old when he is old, and *born* when he is born.

This way of thinking smooths over the apparent contradiction in the Timaeus where Plato indicates that something which was ungenerated was "made" at a specific moment, a "moment," however, which actually exists outside of time. In the same way, one can describe the soul as "older" than all other things or say that something "extra-temporal" existed "before" time. If time is "born," the extra-temporal already existed *when* time was born. According to the *Timaeus,* time (37C) actually *began,* had a point of origin. It is in such terms that the extra-temporal soul can itself be said "to be born."[13]

Muller, on the other hand, is of the opinion that in the *Laws,* soul's creation has no place, as in *Timaeus,* and that the words *protera* and *presbytera* have by no means a temporal sense: "Das ware im Timaios vielleicht möglich, wo mindestens die Seele geschaffen wird; in den Nomoi aber hat die Schöpfung keine Stelle,"[14] and ". . . Daher die Begriffe *protera* und *presbytera* die in den Nomoi keines falls zeitlichen sinn haben."[15]

In addition to the points of view summarized above, other scholars have expressed quite contrary opinions as to the soul's origin. Vlastos, for instance, claims that "the Laws had assumed" the soul's creation "but prudently refrained from presenting it as a problem."[16] In other words he claims, that when Plato wrote the *Laws* he believed the soul to be created, i.e., to have had a beginning.

Prof. Skemp, for his part, charges Plato's commentators with being slow to acknowledge that the soul is a created thing, "except *didaskalias charin*" and this, of course, in virtue of the apparent discrepancy of *Phaedrus* and *Laws*. Further, in a footnote, he observes that *Laws* X speaks of the psyche as created thing at 892C; cf. 892A, 896A and at the "crucial" passage XII 967D.[17]

The late Professor R. Demos in an informative and ingenious article[18] examines "the concept of the soul as the efficient cause of motion, change and all becoming everywhere in the cosmos."[19] His cardinal texts in this exposition are *Sophist* 246A-249D, *The Phaedrus* 245 C. D. and a considerable portion of *Laws,* X.[20] Professor Demos notes that "the paragraph on the soul in the *Phaedrus* (245) is long, extremely involved, extremely compact and extremely difficult."[21] He conjectures that the 245 paragraph is an insertion because it "does not seem to fit the rest of the dialogue."[22] Furthermore, he discusses the obvious contradiction of *Timaeus, Phaedrus* and the *Laws* at some length, concluding "that there is no reconciliation, no solution of the contradiction."[23] Instead, he stresses "the doctrine of the *Phaedrus,* of the *Sophist,* and (partly) of the *Laws,* as a separate and special doctrine of the soul conceived as really real and as a primordial agency of change, even though Plato may not have been consistently faithful to this view."[24]

Although the various attempts at reconciliation are a welcome contribution toward interpreting the antithetical Platonic passages, I personally favor the view that regards the human soul as a created thing; that is, that the individual soul was created by the Platonic God (variously termed Demiurge, Soul as source of motion and life, The Idea of Good) along with time.

In the first place, in *Phaedrus* 245C6-246A2 and in *Laws X,* though Plato speaks both for the divine and the human soul, he emphasizes the soul as a cosmological principle. Secondly, the "eikos-logos" (probable tale) does not necessarily restrict the meaning to an entirely mythical view or fanciful story. As I see it, Plato employs the myth to express certain truths in which he believed.

1. *Timaeus* 35A-B. To this obscure passage "intelligent accounts" are given by the following scholars: A. E. Taylor, *A Commentary on Plato's Timaeus,* Oxford, 1928, pp. 106-136; P. Shorey, "The Timaeus of Plato," *American Journal of Philology,* X, 1889, pp. 51-54; Idem, "Recent interpretations of the Timaeus," Classical Philology, XXIII, 1928, p. 352; G. M. A. Grube, "The Composition of the World-Soul in Timaeus 3 A-B," *Classical Philology,* XXVII, 1932, p. 81; Idem, *Plato's Thought,* London, 1935, pp. 142-143; F. M. Cornford, *Plato's Cosmology* (*The Timaeus of Plato*), London, 1937, 1956, pp. 59-66. Also in Procli Diadochi, in *Platonis Timaeum commentaria,* ed. by E. Diehl, Lipsiae, MCMIV, p. 156.

2. *Ibid.* 42D6-E1-4; 69C3-D1.

3. *Timaeus* 41D4-E2. Comp. *Philebus* 30A. Rene Schaerer, *Dieu. l'homme et la vie d'apres Platon,* Neuchatel, 1944, p. 42, agrees that the human soul retains a small quantity of pure principle but that this principle is now ousted by the Other. Further, ibid. p. 42, n. 1, he illustrates difference in ingredients as follows

La formule de l'âme cosmique est:

$$\text{Meme} + \text{Autre} + \left(\frac{\text{Meme}}{2} + \frac{\text{Autre}}{2}\right)$$

celle de l'âme humaine est:

$$\text{Autre} + \left(\frac{\text{Meme}}{2} + \frac{\text{Autre}}{2}\right)$$

F. Solmsen, *Plato's Theology,* N.Y. 1942, p. 93, is of the opinion that the individual souls are either parts of the Universal Soul or at least of the same stuff. E. W. Simson, *Der Begriff der Seele bei Plato,* p. 85, reviewing what Plato in *Timaeus* writes about the soul's formation, observes in a general way that the material origin of the human soul is the same as that of the World-Soul and that its origin occurred in the same manner as that of the World-Soul.

4. *Laws* 892A4.

5. *Laws* 892C3-8; ibid. 896A-C; ibid. 899C7; ibid. 966D9-10, E1-2; ibid 967D6-7; also Tim. 34C4-5.

6. *Phaedrus* 245C6-246A2.

7. We may note in passing that Plutarch first tried to reconcile the relevant statements in the *Phaedrus* and *Laws* with a literal interpretation of the *Timaeus.* He was, of course, unsuccessful, and his exposition is entirely illogical and untenable. See "De animae procreatione" in Timaeo, 1016C-D, 5-15 in Plutarchi Moralia, Vol. VI, fasc. 1 (ed. by C. Hubert and H. Drexler, Lipsiae in Eadibus B. G. Teubueri MCMLIX, p. 153); see also R. M. Jones, *The Platonism of Plutarch,* pp. 81-85; A. E. Taylor, *A Commentary on Plato's Timaeus,* Oxford, 1962, pp. 117-118; H. Cherniss, *Aristotle's Criticism of Plato and the Academy,* Baltimore, 1944, p. 426, n. 360.

8. *Timaeus* 29 D3. Scholars supporting the mythical exposition are E. Zeller, *Plato and the Older Academy,* N.Y., 1962, p. 405, n. 40; E. Rohde, *Psyche,* London, 1952, p. 479, n. 18; G. Grube, *Plato's Thought,* London, 1935, p. 142; F. M. Cornford, *Plato's Cosmology,* London, 1956, pp. 28-32; F. Solmsen, *Plato's Theology,* Ithaca, 1942, pp. 426, n. 359; 430-431; and A. E. Taylor, *Commentary on Plato's Timaeus,* Oxford, 1962, p. 73; A. E. Taylor, *Plato,* London, 1960, pp. 440-441 gives a somewhat different view. Ernst Howald, "eikos logos" *Hermes* 57, 1922, pp. 63-79, seems to exaggerate considerably (for this reference see also F. Solmsen, ibid., p. 120, n. 32;) R. Hackforth, "Plato's Cosmogony (Timaeus 27D ff)" *Classical Quarterly,* N. S. X, 1959, p. 21; E. W. Simson, *Der Begriff der Seele,* p. 85. It may be noted on the other hand that G. Vlastos, "The disorderly motion." *Classical Quarterly,* XXIII, 1939, pp. 71-83, arguing for a literal interpretation of the pre-cosmical disorderly motion, supports the view that the inconsistencies are "symptomatic of the contradiction inherent in Plato's conception of genesis" and that P. Frutiger, *Mythes de Platon,* Paris, 1930, p. 173 ff, distinguishes two senses of the myth or story; see also F. M. Cornford, *Plato's Cosmology,* pp. 31-32, n. 1.

9. H. Cherniss, *Aristotle's Criticism of Plato and the Academy,* p. 430-1 n. 365; cf. Procli Diadochi in *Platonis Timaeum Commentaria,* ed. by E. Diehl, Lipsiae, MCMIV, Vol. II, 175D11-23 p. 117, whom Cherniss follows in his concluding remarks.

10. H. Cherniss *ibid.* pp. 430-1 n. 365.

11. R. Hackforth, "Plato's Theism," *Classical Quarterly,* XXX Cambridge (1936) p. 5 ff.

12. Idem, *Plato's Phaedrus,* Cambridge (1952) p. 67. It may be of interest to note that in his posthumous article "Plato's Cosmogony," *Classical Quarterly* N. S. IX (1959) p. 21, Hackforth sees Phaedrus' ungenerated soul as "the necessary presupposition of all movements that occur in the Universe, coeval with the Universe."

13. H. D. Rankin, *Plato and the Individual,* pp. 28-9.

14. G. Muller, *Studien zu den Platonischen Nomoi,* Munchen (1951) (in Zetemata, monographien zur Klassischen Altertums-Wissenschaft, Heft 3) p. 86.

15. G. Muller, ibid., p. 85, n. 4.

16. G. Vlastos, "The disorderly motion in the Timaios," *Classical Quarterly,* XXXIII (1939), 79, n. 2 and 82, n. 1; see also H. Cherniss, *Aristotle's Criticism of Plato and the Academy,* p. 430, n. 365.

17. J. B. Skemp, *The Theory of Motion in Plato's later Dialogues,* Cambridge (1942), p. 112, n. 1.

18. "Plato's Doctrine of the Psyche as a Self-Moving Motion," Journal of the History of Philosophy, 6, 1968, 133-145.

19. *Ibid.,* p. 133.

20. *Ibid.,* p. 133.

21. *Ibid.,* p. 134.

22. *Ibid.,* p. 134.

23. *Ibid.,* p. 145.

24. *Ibid.,* p. 145.

25. Further information on Plato's theology is given in Appendix I.

THE DIVISION OF THE SOUL

The statement under consideration could be expressed as follows: Is the human soul simple, of one form or kind, uncompounded,[1] or is it tripartite[2] and composite? In other words, is soul a differentiated unity or a simple unity, or is it both, a one and a many?

The whole question is not without its complexities. Since this is so, and we wish to gain the clearest possible view, then we have to go round a longer way.[3]

Our proposed investigation will therefore fall into the following sections:

1. Origin of the doctrine: Pythagorean or Platonic?
2. Tripartition of the soul:
   a) in the *Republic*
   b) in the *Phaedrus*
   c) in the *Timaeus*
   d) in the other dialogues.
3. Conclusion: proposed solution.

1. Origin of the doctrine: Pythagorean or Platonic?

Although the Pythagoreans did not propound any clear statement about a tripartite soul, some modern scholars nevertheless favour the notion that the origin of the doctrine of the threefold soul is Pythagorean rather than Platonic.

Burnet, for instance, regards the *Phaedo* 68C2 as implying the tripartite division of the soul. He prefers this "somewhat primitive psychology" as being older than Socrates, for it stands in intimate connection with the Famous Pythagorean apologue of the three lives compared to the three classes of men who go to Olympia: 1) to look on, 2) to compete, 3) to buy and sell

(Iambl. *V.P.* 58). In further support of his view, he quotes *Poseidonius* and *Iamblichus*, as saying that the doctrine of the three parts of the soul goes back to Pythagoras himself, that it originally was Pythagorean indeed, and that Plato himself worked out and completed it.[4]

In an excellent article, J. L. Stocks, following Burnet's line of thought, finds it unnecessary to search the records of Greek philosophy for further detailed evidence of the profound and continued influence of the doctrine. He is content to conclude that all probabilities favour the truth of the tradition of its Pythagorean origin.[5]

Cornford, on the other hand, remarks that he is not certain whether the doctrine of the three lives implies a definite division of the soul into three parts. He suggests that the natural impression produced by this passage is that the notion of the three lives was a commonplace but one not necessarily based on a tripartite psychology.[6] Further, he argues that the tripartite psychology has as its final basis a social structure older than Pythagoras himself and that it ultimately does not matter at what date or in whose hands interpretation in terms of psychology took place.[7]

The view that the doctrine of the three parts of the soul is rooted in the Pythagoreans has recently been challenged by two equally eminent scholars, Grube and Hackforth. Professor Grube finds Burnet's and Taylor's interpretation unsatisfactory and faulty. He observes: "Whereas the *Phaedo* (with the Pythagoreans) speaks of three different types of men, in the *Republic* and the *Phaedrus* these become three parts of the same soul."[8] The passions of the philosopher in the *Phaedo* he notes are not parts of his soul.

Professor Hackforth who disagrees also with Burnet and Taylor ascribes along with the late Professor W. Jaegar (*Aristotle,* E. T. 1948[2] p. 98) the origin of the three types of men to the Academy rather than to Pythagoras. Further he rejects the suggestion that the *Republic* IX, 581, has its origin in Pythagoras and rules out Burnet's implication of a tripartite soul on *Phaedo* 68C1-4 and in the whole dialogue as impossible and groundless.[9]

Grube and Hackforth may be right as far as the alleged tripartite soul found by Burnet in the *Phaedo,* but not, I think, regarding the origin of the three types of men which, according to Burnet's evidence, seems to belong to a generation older than that of Plato.

2. The tripartition of the soul: a) in the *Republic*

In the Republic, Plato advances the tentative proposition that the three psychological kinds or forms correspond to the three orders of the city,[10] and proceeds now to consider, whether the three "parts" or better elements or faculties concerned are distinct or identical, the same or different.[11]

Plato, to advance his case, applies first the familiar Law of Contradiction, viz, the general principle "that the same thing cannot act in two opposite ways or be in two opposite states at the same time, with respect to the same part of itself, and in relation to the same object."[12] To illustrate this general principle, he cites the example of the standing man (*Republic* 436C9-11) and the spinning peg-top (436D-E), but the example which best fits his point is that of the thirsty man.[13] Every thirsty man desires to drink,[14] but if there is something which holds him back and forbids him to drink, this something, according to the law of contradiction, must be an element in the soul other than in the thirsty impulse.[15]

So far, Plato has speculated that the elements in the human soul are two, each different and distinct from the other:[16] the rational principle[17] with which the soul reasons and the irrational appetite[18] which is closely connected with pleasure and satisfaction.

Plato next turns his attention to the "spirited" element in the soul which is manifested in indignation and anger.[19] This element differs from desire or appetite and sometimes opposes it.[20] Further, the spirit, although akin to reason and its ally,[21] nevertheless is distinct from it.[22] The fact that the spirit is not identical with the reason can be seen in children and animals, who are full of passionate feelings from their very birth but who never become reasonable,[23] or in the man described by Odysseus who "strikes himself on the chest and calls his heart to order."[24] an instance where one element rebukes another.

Thus, Plato establishes his case and arrives at the conclusion that the same three elements exist in the human soul as in the state.[25]

Plato makes use of this threefold division of the soul on two other occasions, but in rather summary fashion: in the interpretation of the four virtues and in the discussion of pleasure. In the first, wisdom is of the reason[26] and courage of the spirit.[27] Self-control and temperature exist when the elements of spirit and appetite are subordinated to the rational faculty.[28] When the three elements of the mind exist harmoniously and perform their function accordingly, there is justice.[29] Finally, justice is a virtue which is no longer concerned with man's external actions but with his inward self.[30] In discussing pleasure, in Book IX, Plato clearly states that each faculty (element) of the soul not only has its own specific pleasures, its peculiar desires, but at a given point in time may govern the soul.[31]

Earlier, Plato described the soul as constructed of three "parts" or functions. Now, in the course of the discussion of immortality in Book X, he advances a new, extremely sketchy argument. He contends that we cannot think of the true nature of the soul as full of diversity and internal conflicts,[32] as a composite substance,[33] for such a composite entity cannot easily be eternal.[34] He adds that if we want to have as clear a picture as possible of the true nature of the soul, we must view it apart from the body.[35]

The apparent disagreement between the above-mentioned passages and Books IV and IX has been interpreted differently by various scholars who, with the exceptions, arrive at more or less the same conclusion.

For P. Shorey, the question debated by psychologists since Aristotle's name (*Eth. Nic.* 1102a31) to the present day is unimportant and of a secondary nature and consequently does not deserve detailed study and scientific development; it is simply a matter of rhetoric, poetry and point of view. He goes on to say that for some purposes we may describe the elements of the soul as distinct entities, but for others we may again treat them not as separate "parts" but as mere aspects of the same thing. Plato himself was very conscious of ambiguity and on different occasions emphasized the aspect which served his purpose best. Finally, Shorey sees no contradiction at all between the *Republic* 436AB passage and X 611-12 and *Phaedo* 68C, 82C.[36]

Two other eminent scholars, E. Rohde and A. E. Taylor, have offered yet another explanation. Rohde argues that Plato abandoned his conception of the natural trichotomy of the soul into parts, which he gave in the *Republic* and still maintained in the *Phaedrus,* because of "the consideration of its immortality and vocation to intercourse with the Divine, immortal and everlasting."[37] Emotions and passions are due to the communion of the soul with the body, a postulate proved by reason, for if they "were indissolubly linked to the soul the latter could never escape from the cycle of rebirths."[38] If only the logisticon, "as the only independently existing side of the soul,"[39] passes into judgment, it would not be necessary for the incomposite and uniform soul to attempt a new ensomatosis since this "process implies materiality and desire."[40] Taylor similarly suggests that for the philosopher, who earnestly desires the supreme good, who draws nearer and nearer to it every day and "makes progress towards the goal," such a theory of tripartite division is of little importance, incomprehensible in many ways, and "increasingly impossible."[41]

J. Adam, on the other hand, regards the "so-called lower parts" not of the nature of the soul but "only incidental to its association with body," and clings to a simple, uncompounded soul.[42]

The acute critic, Frutiger, applying the traditional interpretation, seems to deny the simplicity of the soul and to favor a differentiated unity, capable of immortality. He rejects the simple soul theory on the following grounds: 1) Plato uses the lengthy negative periphrasis (te alethestate physei) instead of the word monoeides; 2) he takes the trouble to tell us that a composite thing can with difficulty be eternal; and 3) the words (os nyn emin efane e psyche) allude not to Book IV but to Books VII and IX. Further, Frutiger seems to favor a differentiated unity, capable of immortality.[43]

Professor W. K. Guthrie, in a very brief paper, discusses, among other aspects of the soul, the passages *Republic* IV and X, and infers that for Plato the soul, in essence is still simple, and only appears composite as the result of its association with the body.[44]

Frutiger's interpretation of the two passages of the *Republic* as indicating a differentiated unity soul, though it is an ingenious and attractive attempt at reconciliation, does not remove all difficulties. For this reason, we favour the view of those who regard the tripartite theory of the Republic as leading towards a simple unity-soul.[45]

b) in the *Phaedrus*

The tripartite concept occurs also in an extremely sketchy account in the *Phaedrus*. In a myth Plato likens the human soul "to the union of powers in a team"[46] consisting of a winged charioteer and two winged steeds which he is attempting to drive. In the case of gods, both driver and horses are of good and noble breed, but in the case of other species, most particularly men, it is not quite the same. The fact that the charioteer must rule steeds of different strains, one of noble stock and the other of ignoble, makes his task difficult indeed, not to say wearisome and unmanageable.[47] In this allegory the charioteer clearly stands for the reason, the horse of good stock for the spirited element, and the horse of bad stock for the irrational appetite.

A few pages later Plato uses this analogy to elucidate the conflict within the soul of the lover-charioteer. In this struggle, the good horse, the lover of honour and glory combined with modesty and temperance, needs no whip but is controlled by command and reason; its fellow, on the contrary, deaf, hot-blooded and the companion of insolence and wantonness, is conquered only with great effort and force through the use of whip and spur.[48] Now the new and startling point which Plato makes here is the attribution of the lower "parts" to the discarnate soul as well.[49]

We might pass over the tripartite theory of the discarnate soul rather quickly on the grounds that the setting of 246A-253C-254E is "a myth, and rigid exactitude of doctrine is not to be expected";[50] yet, several critics have dealt with the problem, and it is useful to recapitulate their views.

Taylor categorically rejects the idea that all three parts are present not only in the discarnate souls, but in the souls of the gods who are never embodied at all. His reasons are that such a doctrine would be at variance with the hints given in the *Republic* and the express teaching of the *Timaeus*. Further, he holds that metaphysical theories can not be built on a mythical base.[51]

Wilamowitz, on the other hand, observes that the picture of the charioteer of the soul, complicated as it is, was meant to represent the condition of the soul only when human life is at its best. He finds the Divine Soul in the *Phaedrus* equally complex.[52]

Hackforth argues that Plato wavers to the end between two conceptions of the soul: the Orphic-Pythagorean notion of soul, divine and complete, free from all physical functions, and the scientific conception of soul as self-mover and source for the motion of other things too.[53] Contrary to A. E. Taylor and Wilamowitz,[54] Hackforth goes on to say that the explicit statement of the *Phaedrus* about the tripartition of the human soul, before and after its incarnation, must be taken "as seriously meant."[55]

Guthrie, in a recent article, poses a different solution.[56] He points to Empedocles as a source for the complex eschatological system of Plato. In these terms, the soul is seen as essentially divine but involved in a reincarnational cycle as a "punishment for sin" — although the nature of the sinfulness is left rather vague. The *Phaedrus* asserts that this "sin" has cost the soul its purity and goes on to describe how it spends ten thousand years circling the cycle of punishment from which it cannot be released unless it succeeds in living the philosophic life for three successive incarnations. The point is made, however, that a thousand years elapse between the beginning of one incarnation and that of the next; consequently, the greater part of the cycle is actually spent in a discarnate state. This arrangement makes it impossible to identify the soul's "impurity" entirely with its incarnate condition, for during the "inter-incarnational" period the soul is still tainted with the stain of the "sin" which imprisoned it within the circuits of the wheel. The concept of immortality thus assumes shape quite distinct from a mere opposition between imprisonment of the soul within a body and release of the soul from thralldom to the body.

Rather the disability which binds the soul is from within, and the soul would never experience bodily existence if it had not by prior sin incurred the punishment of incarnation. Here it is important to note immortality gains a moral meaning, and no longer implies mere durability.

Guthrie does not accept the common notion that the psychology of the *Phaedo* denies the survival in the discarnate state of the lower parts of the soul – a survival which the *Phaedrus*, per contra, asserts. He admits that the *Phaedo* declares these lower parts to be no true attribute of the soul's proper nature, but emphasizes that we are then told "that a soul that has given itself over to bodily desires and pleasures while in the body is, when it leaves it, still permeated by the corporeal." This view is found again in the *Gorgias*, where we learn that the soul is marked inescapably with the character of the life led by the body, a character which, however well it has been disguised by the body, becomes known beyond any pretence or concealment on death, and on that basis is the soul judged.

Guthrie finds no contradiction between the statements of the *Phaedo* and Plato's other references to the matter and finds it "particularly difficult to agree" with Hackforth's conclusion, that "even 'pure' soul is thymoeides and epithymetikos as well as logistikos," for Guthrie sees the end of the philosophic life to reach beyond such taints, beyond the grip of the wheel; to become "like unto a god," thus regaining the soul's original condition.

Plato's imagery, Guthrie maintains, is aimed at describing a state of affairs which is known empirically, viz., that the nature of man is mixed, and good and evil are both present. Such imagery then, cannot be used to explain this fact or to indicate the origin of the evil admixture. Neither can it be adduced to suggest that the content of the image – the charioteer and the team of horses – necessarily implies anything about the nature of the souls of the gods themselves and whether their souls, like these of men, are peccable. Plato, like Empedocles, is concerned with the effects of the condition of sinfulness rather than with the source of that condition. Guthrie concludes that Plato turned to a myth as the best illustration of a religious truth which he passionately believed, "but of which neither he nor any other man can give a rational explation."[57]

c) In the *Timaeus*

Timaeus's account of the triplicity of the soul, fascinating and fanciful as it is, runs in many respects along the same lines as the presentation in the *Republic*.[58] Here Plato declares that only the rational part, *anima rationalis,* was created by the Demiurge out of the same ingrendients as the world soul.[59] This part is located in the head[60] and alone enjoys the privilege of being immortal.[61] Further, he speaks of the mortal parts of the soul, together with the body itself, as made by the celestial gods.[62]

Now, the apparent bipartition, immortal-divine and mortal, becomes tripartite through the analysis of the mortal into spirited and appetitive elements.[63] The spirited element, on the one hand, is situated between the midriff and the neck, that is, in the heart;[64] and the appetitive one is placed in the belly, viz., below the midriff.[65]

Plato concludes that what has been said is merely provisional and would be an accurate, scientific statement if only a god would have confirmed it.[66]

d) In the other *dialogues*

We have been dealing with the threefold theory of the human soul as it is set forth most fully in the *Republic* and *Timaeus* and in the imposing allegory of the *Phaedrus*. There remains something to be said about the doctrine with reference to the *Phaedo*, the *Statesman* and the *Laws*. In the *Phaedo* we cannot trace, I believe, a soul's division, for Plato clearly speaks of a simple, uniform, incomposite and immortal soul.[67] In the *Statesman* only a vague distinction between a divine and a human or animal element of the soul occurs.[68] It is only concerning the *Laws* that an element of controversy has arisen.

As far as the division of the soul in the *Laws* is concerned, Plato says nothing explicit; notwithstanding, D. A. Rees distinguishes a bipartition and T. J. Saunders a tripartition of the soul in the *Laws*. Dr. Rees, referring mainly to *Laws* IX 863E-864A, 626E, 630A-B, 689A-E, 696C, 840-C, *Magna Moralia* I, 1182A 213 ff, *Protrepticus, Nic. Eth.* IV, 1168B28–1169A3, X, 1177B31–1178A3, *Nic. Eth.* I, 13, 1102A26-28 and *De Anima* III 432Q24-26, claims that "the *Laws* does in fact suggest a bipartition of the soul more naturally than a tripartition, as is confirmed by IX, 863E-864A."[69] Saunders, citing the same passages and adding 869E, 93A, 731AB, 717D, 770D and 783A, reaches the general conclusion that the soul in the *Laws* can be analysed into the three elements equivalent to those described in the *Republic*.[70] One cannot, I might add, expect precision in these general considerations,[71] in spite of the fact that both papers are informative, interesting and ingenious, for the simple reason that in the *Laws* there is no one single clear statement about the threefold soul as in the other dialogues (*Republic, Timaeus, Phaedrus*).

3. Conclusion: proposed solution

The problem of the tripartite soul is indeed "amongst the thorniest of all Platonic problems."[72] In reply to the opening question, whether the soul is simple and incomposite or composite and compound, we may now generally conclude that the human soul, is, in its true nature, incomposite, uncompounded and simple, and that the so-called lower two parts or elements are not distinct or real parts but are, on the contrary, its temporary and transitory manifestations. These aspects owe their own existence to corporeality, lasting only as long as the soul is related to the body.[73]

Our preference for a simple and uncompounded soul with mental energies and activities, while it is connected with the body, is based on the following reasons:

1. Such a view elucidates more satisfactorily the relation of soul to body and the immortality of the soul.

2. Plato himself does not use a word denoting "part" in a literal, material sense. On the contrary, he employs such terms as *eide* in 435B2, C1,5, E2, 439E2 and *gene* in 441C4, 443D5, in a metaphorical and convenient way to signify forms or functions or principles of action.[74] The word *meros* is used when the whole tripartite discussion comes to an end, and only once in 442B11 and B3, where it cannot be literally translated as "part," a meaning which does not suit the context but rather as "element" or "factor." After all, we must bear in mind that Plato never developed a precise terminology.[75]

3. We might well remind ourselves of Plato's warning that his accounts concerning the tripartite soul are provisional and tentative and that scientific precision must not be expected.[76]

4. It should be noted that Plato's main concern here is ethical and political theory, not psychology itself, as a special branch of science, or the scientific analysis of the mind. He found the tripartite division of the soul helpful and, according to the context, adapted the doctrine in each dialogue to suit his purpose.[77]

Finally, it might be said that some scholars regard the tripartite concept as a "popular, non-scientific" doctrine,[78] a "mythic" one,[79] "of little importance,"[80] and consequently "too much reliance should not be placed" on it.[81]

1. *Phaedo* 78C4-7, 80B1-4 *Republic* 611B1-8.

2. Cf. *Republic* IV, 435C5, 435C-441; 611B-612A; also Phaedrus, 246A ff; *Tim.* 69C-72D.

3. *Republic* 435D4-5.

4. J. Burnet, *Plato's Phaedo,* Oxford (1959), n. on 68C2; Idem, *Early Greek Philosophy,* p. 98, cf. 296 n. 2; Idem., *Greek Philosophy,* London, 1930, pp. 42 n. 2 and 177; A. E. Taylor, *A Commentary on Plato's Timaeus,* pp. 497-8 and n. 1; Idem, *Plato; the Man and his Work,* p. 231 n. 1 and W. F. R. Hardie, *A Study in Plato,* Oxford (1936), p. 138, move in the same direction by maintaining the Pythagorean origin of the doctrine; C. J. Classen, *Sprachliche deutung als tribkraft Platonischen und Sokratichen Philosophierens,* (1959), Munich, p. 21 n. 4, on the other hand, referring to the above scholars, notes that "bestehen auf Pythagoreischen nosprung der Dreiteilung der Seele."

5. J. L. Stocks, "Plato and the Tripartite of the Soul;" *Mind* XXIV (1915) London, 209, 210 and 219.

6. F. M. Cornford, "Psychology and Social Structure in the Republic of Plato," The *Classical Quarterly,* VI (1912), p. 247 n. 2.

7. F. M. Cornford, Ibid., p. 247, n. 2.

8. G. M. A. Grube, *Plato's Thought,* p. 133, n. 1.

9. R. Hackforth, *Plato's Phaedo,* Cambridge, 1955, p. 56 n. 1. Here Hackforth, n. 4, in support of his opinion, cites Frutiger, *Mythes de Platon,* pp. 77 ff; G. Grube, *Plato's Thought,* p. 133; E. R. Dodds, *The Greeks and the Irrational,* California, 1951, pp. 227 f.

10. *Republic* 434D-435E. On the parallelism between state and soul and especially on the question of whether the tripartition of state or soul is prior: F. M. Cornford, "Psychology and social structure in the Republic of Plato," *Classical Quarterly* (1912) VI, pp. 247-265, maintains that the division of the state came first; R. Hackforth, "The Modification of Plan in Plato's Republic," *Classical Quarterly* (1913) VII, p. 265, who replies to Cornford's assertion and believes "Plato to have had a tripartite psychology in his mind from the beginning of Book II — a psychology, indeed, which is prior to the building up of the political structure"; R. C. Cross and A. D. Woozley, *Plato's Republic,* London (1964) pp. 130-2 who are of the same opinion as Hackforth; C. J. Classen, *Sprachliche deutung als Triebkraft,* pp. 22-23, who argues, that the problem worth solving is not where the tripartition first appears, but where the parallel between state and soul has its origin. On the question in general one may also consult E. G. Ballard, "Plato's movement from an ethics of the individual to a science of particulars," *Tulane Studies in Philosophy,* Vol. VI (Studies in Ethics), Tulane University, New Orleans (1957) pp. 14, 15-16 and more particularly the excellent article of the late H. W. B. Joseph, "Plato's Republic: the comparison between the soul and the state," in *Essays in Ancient and Modern Philosophy,* Oxford (1935), pp. 82-121.

11. *Republic* 436B5-6.
12. *Ibid.* 436B8-9 and 436E9-10; trans, F. M. Cornford, *The Republic of Plato,* p. 128.
13. *Republic* 437B7-439D.
14. *Ibid.,* 439A9-439B1.
15. *Ibid.,* 439B3-6.
16. *Republic* 439D4-5.
17. *Ibid.,* 439D5.
18. *Ibid.,* 439D6-8.
19. *Ibid.,* 439E3
20. *Ibid.,* 439E6-440D.
21. *Ibid.,* 440E5.
22. *Ibid.,* 440E8-10—441A1-6.
23. *Ibid.,* 441A7-10—441B1-3.
24. *Republic* 441B4-441C1-3; Homer, *Odysseus,* Book XX, 17; in W. W. Merry, Oxford, MDCCCCI, p. 126, n. on XX, 17, p. 124 and in H. C. P. Lee, *Plato, the Republic,* p. 193 n. 1.
25. *Ibid.,* 441C5-7.
26. *Ibid.,* 441E4-5; 442C6-10.
27. *Ibid.,* 441E; 442C1-4.
28. *Ibid.,* 442C10-11; D1-2.
29. *Ibid.,* 442C10-11C; 444E.
30. *Republic,* 443C9-10, D ff.
31. *Ibid.,* 580D6-8; also in 581C5.
32. *Ibid.,* 611B1-3.
33. *Ibid.,* 611B5-6; cf. *Phaedo* 78C; Plotinus, *Enneades* I, 1, 12, plotini, opera, Tomus I, ed. by P. Henry & H. R. Schwyzer, Paris (1951).
34. *Ibid.,* 611B5.
35. *Ibid.,* 611B10-C1-2 ff; *Phaedo* 82E, 83D-E, 81C.
36. P. Shorey, *Plato, the Republic,* N.Y. (1930) in LCL, Vol. I, pp. 380-1 n. d; Idem, *Unity of Plato's Thought,* pp. 42-3; Idem, *What Plato Said,* the University of Chicago Press, (1962), p. 563 n. on 435BC, where Shorey reformulates the same observations and provides references in the various dialogues for non-contradiction.
37. E. Rohde, *Psyche,* p. 481, n. 29.
38. *Ibid.,* p. 481, n. 29.
39. *Ibid.,* p. 481, n. 29.
40. *Ibid.,* p. 481, n. 29.
41. A. E. Taylor, *Plato, the Man and His Work,* pp. 281-282 and n. 1.
42. J. Adam, *Plato's Republic,* Cambridge, 1963, II, p. 426 on 611B v. 8; *Ibid.,* p. 427 on 611 v. 12; *Ibid.,* p. 428 on 611D v. 30; *Ibid.,* p. 429 on 612A v. 3.
43. P. Frutiger, *Les Mythes de Platon,* Paris (1930) p. 93. It should be noted also that Dr. R. H. Hall, *Plato and the Individual,* pp. 150-1, The Hague, 1963, obviously influenced by Frutiger, insists that a careful analysis of the passage (X 611B-612A) reveals that there is a fundamental consistency between it and the account in Book IV, if we regard both as presenting at least as probable an account of the soul as a complex or differentiated unity.
44. W. K. C. Guthrie, "Plato's views on the nature of the soul" in *Recherches sur la tradition Platonicienne, in Entretiens sur l'antiquité classique,* Tome III, Geneve (1955) pp. 6-7.

45. More reasons for this view are given below in the general conclusion of the whole tripartite problem.

46. R. Hackforth, *Plato's Phaedrus,* p. 67; A. E. Taylor, *Plato,* p. 307, n. 1, comments on *Phaedrus* 246A6-7 as follows: "forming a single living whole. . . . It is inserted in order to insist on the unity of the individual mind. We are to think of the driver and his horses as a single organism."

47. Phaedrus, 246A5-B4.

48. *Phaedrus,* 253-254E.

49. *Ibid.,* 246A-E, 248C-249D.

50. D. A. Rees, "Bipartition of the soul in the early Academy," *Journal of Hellenic Studies,* LXXVII (1) (1957) p. 112.

51. A. E. Taylor, *Plato,* p. 307.

52. U. von Wilamowitz, *Platon,* Berlin, 1919, I, p. 467.

53. G. E. L. Owen, "The Place of the *Timaeus* in Plato's Dialogues," *Classical Quarterly,* N. S. Vol. III, 1953, p. 95 takes the view that "the contradiction in *Timaeus, Phaedrus,* 246A ff and *Laws* 897A is apparent and not real." He further makes the point that we avoid the conclusion that Plato "wavered to the end" between these alternatives, if we set the *Phaedrus* after the *Timaeus.*

54. See Taylor, ibid., p. 307 and Wilamowitz, ibid., p. 467.

55. R. Hackforth, *Plato's Phaedrus,* p. 76 n. 33.

56. W. K. C. Guthrie, "Plato's Views on the Nature of the Soul," in Recherches sur la Tradition Platonicienne, in Entretiens sur l'antiquité Classique, Tome III, Geneve, 1955, pp. 10-14.

57. W. K. C. Guthrie, "Plato's views on the nature of the soul" in *Recherches sur la tradition Platonicienne, in Entretiens sur l'antiqué classique,* Tome III, pp. 10-14.

58. A. E. Taylor, *A Commentary on Plato's Timaeus,* p. 496 n. on 69C7, finds Timaeus's teaching of the threefold soul to correspond precisely to that of the *Republic,* with the difference, of course, that the inferior two parts are mortal and located in the body.

59. *Timaeus* 41D4-E1; 69B8-C1-3; comp. also 34BC and 90A5-8.

60. *Ibid.,* 44D4-6; 45A1-2; 69D6-7, E1.

61. *Ibid.,* 44D5-6; 45A1-2; 69C5-6; 69D5; 69D6; 90A1-9.

62. *Ibid.,* 42D6-E1-4; 69C3-D1.

63. Aristotle, *Eth. Nic.* 1, 13, 10, prefers the bipartition.

64. *Timaeus* 70A-D6.

65. *Ibid.,* 70D7-E1-3; the appetitive form belongs also to trees, plants and seeds, see *Timaeus* 77-AB.

66. *Ibid.,* 72D4-8; comp. also *Phaedrus* 246A1-4 and *Republic* 435CD.

67. *Phaedo* 78C1 and 80B1-3; with regard to Phaedo's teaching on the triplicity of the soul, some scholars argue as follows: R. H. Archer-Hind, (Platonos Phaedon) *The Phaedo of Plato,* London (1894) pp. XXXIII, XXXIV-V, opposes the division of the soul in general and particularly here (in *Phaedo*) and favours the simple and uniform soul. He rejects the lower "parts" as different and adopts the milder expression "modes of the soul's activity"; Wilamowitz, *Platon,* I, p. 341, suggests that Plato wanted to avoid overloading his exposition; P. Shorey, *The Unity of Plato's Thought,* and W. K. C. Guthrie, "Plato's views on the nature of the soul" in *Recherches sur la tradition Platonicienne, in Entretiens sur l'antiquité classique,* p. 12, maintain that Phaedo (79BCE ff) does not affirm that the soul is simple and uncompounded but that the body is

more akin to the composite and the soul to the simple and unchanging; P. Frutiger, *Myths de Platon,* p. 77, on the other hand, holds that the soul was composed of three parts, of which one only was immortal. He would certainly not have given to this last the generic name of *psyche* nor passed in silence completely over the other two (". . . ni passe les deux autres entrierement sous silence"); R. Hackforth, *Plato's Phaedo,* pp. 11-12, notes that the simplicity and incomposite nature of the soul is categorically asserted in the dialogue of the *Phaedo.*

68. *Statesman* 309C1-3. J. B. Skemp, *Plato's Statesman,* London (1952) pp. 223, n. 1; 229, n. 1 and 239, observes that the tripartite psychology "is explicitly supplanted in the Politicus." His view is supported by J. Gould, *The Development of Plato's Ethics,* Cambridge (1955), pp. 214-5 G. E. L. Owen, *Mind,* N. S. 62 (1953) p. 272 and J. Tate, *Classical Review,* N. S. 4 (1954) p. 116, reviewing Skemp's book, speak against this assertion.

69. D. A. Rees, "Bipartition of the Soul in the Early Academy," *Journal of Hellenic Studies,* LXXVII (1), 1957, pp. 112-118, especially p. 116. See also his later paper "Theories of the Soul in the Early Aristotle" in *Aristotle and Plato in the Mid-Fourth Century,* ed. by I. Düring and G. E. L. Owen, Göteborg, 1960, pp. 196-197, where he argues "that there are also traces in Plato of a tendency towards a bipartition of the soul, distinguishing one element which is rational and immortal and another which is irrational and mortal." (*Republic* X 608d ff, *Timaeus* 65a, 72d, *Politicus* 309c). With reference to the *Laws* Dr. Rees writes: "While the *Laws* carefully avoids committing itself definitely either to a bipartition or to a tripartition, the crucial passage being IX863b, where it is left undetermined whether *thymos is a meros* of the soul or a *pathos,* the moral psychology of the dialogue being interpretable either in a bipartite sense or in tripartite."

70. T. J. Saunders, "Soul and State in Plato's Laws," *Eranos,* Vol. LX, 1962, 37-55 (p. 41 here). See also C. Ritter, *Platon,* Vol. II, Munchen, 1910, p. 451, who refers to I. 644C IX. 863B and notes that the *Laws* treats the soul as tripartite. Ritter does not succeed in his argument, as neither passage proves his point. Cf. also Rees, *op. cit.,* p. 112.

71. This point seems to be admitted by both Rees (pp. 113 and particularly 115) and Saunders (pp. 38 and 41).

72. R. Hackforth, *Plato's Phaedrus,* p. 75.

73. A view of a simple and incomposite soul with mental expressions or impulses and motives, spiritual functions and tendencies is strongly and consistently held by others: R. D. Archer-Hind, "On some difficulties in the Platonic psychology," *Journal of Philology,* Vol. X (1882), pp. 129-31; J. Adam, *Republic,* II, p. 426 n. on 611B8; 427 on 611B12; p. 429 on 612A3; J. L. Stock's "Plato and the tripartite of the Soul," *Mind,* XXIV (1915) p. 218; U. V. Wilamowitz, *Platon,* Berlin (1919) I, p. 470; C. Ritter, *Platon,* Munich (1910) I, pp. 226-7; E. Zeller, *Plato and the Older Academy,* pp. 389-90; P. Shorey, *Unity of Plato's Thought,* p. 42; A. E. Taylor, *The Mind of Plato* (paperback) Michigan (1960) pp. 80, 83; F. M. Cornford, "The Division of the Soul," in *Hibbert Journal,* XXVIII (1920-30) pp. 213-5; Idem. *The Doctrine of Eros, The Unwritten Philosophy,* Cambridge (1950), p. 71; J. Theodorakopoulos, *Eisagoge sto Phaedro,* Athens, 1948, p. 8; H. Gaus, *Philosophischer Handkommentar zu den Dialogen Platos,* Bern (1952), I/1 p. 143; H. D. P.

Lee, *Plato, the Republic* p. 184; W. K. C. Guthrie, "Plato's views on the nature of the soul," in *Recherches sur la Tradition Platonicienne, in Entretiens sur l'antiquité classique,* pp. 18-19.

74. N. R. Murphy, *The Interpretation of Plato's Republic,* Oxford (1960), p. 36; also in J. Gould, *The Development of Plato's Ethics,* Cambridge (1955), p. 151, n. 2.

75. H. W. B. Joseph, *Essays Ancient and Modern,* p. 48, remarks that "Plato is not pedantically rigid in his use of terms."

76. *Timaeus* 72D4-7; *Phaedrus* 246A3-6; *Republic* 435CD ff.

77. It should be observed that the following scholars strongly emphasize that point: P. Shorey, *The Unity of Plato's Thought,* pp. 42-43 (168-169); Idem, *Plato's Republic,* LCL, p. 381 n.d.; Idem, *What Plato Said,* p. 563 n. on 43BC; W. Jaeger, *Paideia: The Ideals of Greek Culture,* Vol. II, Oxford, 1944, pp. 199 ff, 400 n. 6; A. E. Taylor, *A Commentary on Plato's Timaeus,* p. 496 n. on 69C7; G. Grote, *Plato and Other Companions of Socrates,* London, 1897, Vol. II, p. 160; C. Ritter, *Platon,* I. 227; P. Frutiger, *Mythes de Platon,* p. 81 n. 1; F. Copleston, *A History of Philosophy,* London, 1961, I, p. 210.

78. A. E. Taylor, *A Commentary on Plato's Timaeus,* p. 497 n. on 69C7; Idem, *Plato,* p. 281.

79. P. Frutiger, *Mythes de Platon,* p. 96.

80. R. C. Cross and A. D. Wooszley, *Plato's Republic,* London, 1964, p. 127.

81. W. F. R. Hardie, *A Study in Plato,* Oxford, 1936, p. 138. E. Zeller, *Plato and the Older Academy,* p. 417, and R. Hackforth, *Plato's Phaedrus,* p. 75, are of the opinion that the theory of the division of the soul remained unresolved in Plato's mind.

SOUL-BODY: THEIR RELATIONSHIP

The psychological dualism of Plato corresponds to his metaphysical dualism.[1] In the *Phaedo* he maintains that the soul in every way resembles the invisible, the immaterial and everlasting world, while the body has much more affinity with the visible and belongs to the material world.[2]

Although we will deal here most particularly with the soul-body relationship, we might add in passing a note about the body itself, as it is described in Platonic dialogues. The body, it is said, is made up of four elements or kinds: Earth, Fire, Water and Air.[3] Thus it shares the common characteristics of this world and is very like it, viz., liable to death and dissolution, manifold, unintelligent, changing and never constant.[4]

Concerning the relation of soul to body, we should note the following. Whereas the soul gives to the body the power to breathe and is the cause of its living and its reviving force,[5] the body, on the other hand, is represented in the dialogues as the prison-house or tomb of the soul. In it, the soul is buried in the present life; there it undergoes punishment for any misdeed; and in it, it remains until the penalty is paid.[6] In addition, Plato writes that the body is the source of evil and exerts an evil influence upon the soul. Further, the body and its appetites cause disturbance and confusion to the soul; they prevent its acquisition of truth and wisdom and its pursuit of true being.[7] Finally, the body and its appetites not only act as perpetual impediments to the higher activities of the soul, which they fill with passions, desires, fears, imaginations of all sorts and foolishness, but they are also the real cause of war, discord and strife.[8] While Plato expressly attributes desires, passions, fears, wars and the like to the body and its appetites,[9] in the *Philebus*, where he develops the doctrine of the bodily pleasures and pains most fully,[10] he quite openly contradicts himself and characteristically remarks that "it is to the soul that all impulse and desire, and indeed the determining principle of the whole creature, belong."[11] Again, we are faced with a real or apparent contradiction, an issue which has been taken up by a number of schools.

Hackforth notes two essential points in his discussion of *Philebus* 35B: In the first place,

> Plato here wished to correct any misconceptions which might have arisen regarding the role which both soul and body play in pleasure and desire. Secondly, though he speaks of pleasure, pain and even desire as physical events in the *Philebus*,[12] he seems to imply quite the opposite; namely, that desire, pleasure, and pain are located in the body, are bodily experiences, and reach the soul through the body.[13]

Shorey, however, sees no contradiction at all in so far as the nature and seat of desire, pleasure and pain are concerned and reminds us of Plato's statement that only a careless or captious reader would misunderstand him.[14] He further defends his case by citing various Platonic passages.[15] Finally, Shorey concludes that the bodily states produce pleasure and pain only when they cross the threshold of consciousness.[16]

Archer-Hind similarly finds no disagreement between *Phaedo* 66D and *Philebus* 35CD, holding that the discrepancy is only apparent and easily reconcilable. In the *Phaedo,* desire, pleasure and pain are attributed to the body as the result of the conjunction between soul and body; in the *Philebus* Plato ascribes them more precisely to the soul because they are an affection of the soul through the body.[17]

A natural inference seems to follow this examination, and that is, that Plato thinks of the body in general as the tomb, prison-house, enemy of the soul, and finally as its source of evil, disorder and corruption.[18]

1. *Phaedo* 79A7-8.
2. *Ibid.*, 79B16-17.
3. *Timaeus* 82A2-3; also in *Timaeus* 42E5-43A1-6.
4. *Phaedo* 80B3-5; *Phaedo* 106E5-6; *Cratyl* 399E1-2; *Axiochus* 365E5.
5. *Cratyl* 399D11-12, E1-3; *Phaedo* 105C9-10, D-15.
6. *Cratyl* 400B10; cf. also with *Gorg.* 493A3; *Phaedo* 82E, 91E8, 92; *Phaedrus* C5-6; and the apocryphal *Axiochus* 365E5-366A; Prof. G. Ryle, The Concept of Mind, London, 1949, p. 15, calls this relationship "the Ghost in the Machine" or "a horse in a locomotive" qtd. in A. Koestler, The Ghost in the Machine, MacMillan Co., N.Y., 1967, pp. 202, 357.
7. *Phaedo* 66A4-7; 66C1-2; 66D5-7; 79C.
8. *Phaedo* 66C2-8; *Republic* 611C1-2, 611D; *Timaeus* 86B-87B and also 82AB. For a full discussion of *Timaeus*, see 86B-87B section, which is not without its intricacies; see A. E. Taylor, *A Commentary on Plato's Timaeus*, pp. 589 ff and more specifically pp. 610-18; F. M. Cornford, *Plato's Cosmology*, pp. 343-9.
9. See ftn. 8.
10. The above doctrine is expounded also in *Republic* IX (583B-587C); *Timaeus* 64A-65B; *Gorg.* 493B-494E; *Phaedo* 60B3-C7, 66C A. E. Taylor, *A Commentary on Plato's Timaeus*, pp. 445-65, deals with this doctrine at some length; F. M. Cornford, *Plato's Cosmology*, pp. 266-9, makes some very brief remarks as well.
11. *Philebus* 35D1-3, trans. R. Hackforth, *Plato's Examination of Pleasure* (*The Philebus*), Cambridge (1945), p. 67.
12. 35D1-3 and 55B1-3; other passages of the same dialogue, 45A, 46B and cf. 41C and especially in the *Republic*, 584C (similarly) Aristotle speaks of bodily pleasure *E. N.* 1104b5, 1154a8, cf. 1173b7-13).
13. R. Hackforth, *Plato's Examination of Pleasure* (*The Philebus*), Cambridge, 1945, p. 61.
14. P. Shorey, *The Unique of Plato's Thought*, pp. 45-46 or 171-172, n. 328, 330, 333.
15. *Ibid.*, *Philebus* 33, 34, 43B, C. cf. *Republic* 462C, 548C, cf.; *Laws* 673A; *Timaeus* 451 and again *Philebus* 39D, 45B; *Phaedo* 65A; *Timaeus* 64A; *Republic* 548C, 485D; *Philebus* 45A, 41C, 436C, 33D; *Timaeus* 64ABC; *Theat* 186C.
16. P. Shorey, *The Unity of Plato's Thought*, pp. 45-46 or 171-172, n. 328, 330, 333.
17. R. D. Archer-Hind, "On Some Difficulties in the Platonic Psychology," *The Journal of Philology*, 1882, X pp. 130-131.
18. R. C. Lodge, *Plato's Theory of Ethics*, London, 1928, pp. 175-216, produces a different and startling theory of the nature and interrelation of soul and body which he characterises as "thoroughly Platonic." The central points of his theory are:

(1) the nature of the body as an instrument, as adapted to spiritual purposes;

(2) the function of the soul as director of the body to the spiritual ends; and

(3) soul and body being regarded as correlates. In his effort to interpret the Platonic passages in such a way in order to suit his purpose, it seems to me that Prof. Lodge misinterprets them and goes too far in his conclusions.

IMMORTALITY OF THE SOUL

There are two important considerations in discussing the problem of the immortality of the soul.

1. The doctrine of the immortality of the soul, as it is set forth principally in the *Phaedo, Republic,* and *Phaedrus* and very briefly and quite incidentally in some of the other dialogues.
2. Whether Plato proves his case, namely that the soul survives death and continues to be intelligent and to exist in some consciousness after the death of the individual.[1]

a) Immortality in the *Phaedo*

Plato, as is well known, discusses particularly the soul's immortality in the *Phaedo.* In order to give a rational explanation to the matter he uses the following arguments: the first argument – generation from the opposites (70A-72E); the second argument – recollection (72E-78A); the third argument – from the affinities (78B-84B); the final argument – the reality of forms (102B-107A) to prove the soul's immortality.

First argument: generation from opposites (70A-72E)

This argument rests on what is known as the cycle theory or theory of opposites. According to this theory everything in nature is in constant change; that is to say, in nature there is continuous process of alteration: all things come into being out of their opposites, the larger out of the smaller, the better out of the worse, the stronger out of the weaker, waking out of sleeping, or vice versa. This principle, Plato argues, is applicable to the living and the dead. If life springs from death, or vice versa, then clearly soul must exist in the world beyond.[2]

Second argument: recollection (72E-78A)

Learning, according to Plato, is basically recollection, that is, our knowledge and understanding are the result not of the sense-experience but of what the soul has known before entering its earthly body. To illustrate his point Plato refers to the knowledge of the idea of equality, beauty, good, justice and holiness. The recollection argument implies that the soul existed before birth and possesses intelligence.[3] Further, Plato says that the existence of forms, of absolute entities and of the soul before its incarnation is interrelated, the two propositions must stand or fall together.[4]

Plato, to complete his argument that the soul exists after death, recalls the argument of opposites.[5]

Third argument: from the affinities (78B-84B)

Since Plato refers us to the soul's affinities to universals, to laws and spiritual principles, to his famous theory of Ideas, let us see how he develops the soul's relation to the Forms.

While composite things are liable to be split into their component parts, incomposite things are not. Again, composite things are mutable; incomposite ones are constant and unchanging. Socrates adds that things which never admit of alteration or undergo any change whatsoever are the Forms, which, at the same time, are invisible and intelligible in contrast to the particular things of the world, which are ever changing and never constant. This conclusion leads Socrates to distinguish between two classes of things — visible and invisible — a distinction which helps Cebes to agree with Socrates, that the soul is akin to and belongs to the invisible class and the body to the visible.[6]

Further, when the soul seeks truth all by itself, it passes to that other world of pure, immortal and imperishable Forms; it always remains there and comes in close and constant contact with these unchanging realities. Cebes admits that this is another reason which forces us to believe that the soul resembles and is akin to the everlasting and unchanging being.

Between the third and the fourth argument, Plato discusses Simmias's and Cebes's objections and the reply of Socrates. Simmias's and Cebes's objections, broadly speaking, are mechanistic in nature, or similar to behavioristic and to the contemporary physiological theories. Simmias sees the soul as an "attunement" of the body, an expression or function of the body. Cebes, on the other hand, disagrees, speaking of the soul as stronger and longer-lived than the body. Both, however, reject the notion of immortality. They do not accept the theory that soul survives death. They both believe that the soul disappears and perishes when we die.[7] Socrates finds Simmias's view incompatible with the theory of recollection, on the one hand, and Cebes's position, on the other hand, insufficient and inapplicable, because it reminds him of the mechanistic explanation (causes-events); instead, he advances a teleological explanation, that of the forms-cause, which is the true explanation of the nature of things and forms the basis for the final argument.[8]

Final argument: reality of forms (102B-107A)

The last argument, relatively long and with its difficulties as it stands, is based also on the existence of the Forms and can be expressed briefly as follows:

Socrates proves by means of analogies (tallness-shortness, hot-cold, snow-fire, even-odd) that opposites exclude each other and cannot coalesce with one another or arise out of one another. In other words, neither a transcendent idea or a form-copy, an immanent character, can take upon itself the nature of its opposite.[9] He then goes on to apply this already established principle, arguing that life is a necessary concomitant of the presence of a soul, the vehicle of life; for soul is, by definition, that which gives life to the body. Since death is the opposite of life and since the soul excludes its opposite, it will not admit death and we may call it immortal, deathless.[10] Plato, discussing a further point, that of imperishability or indestructibility[11] in the remainder of the present argument, infers categorically and firmly that the soul is deathless, immortal and imperishable and that our souls will exist in the other world.[12]

With reference to the preceding arguments for immortality in the Phaedo, perhaps it may be said that they are not true scientific proofs and are puzzling and difficult to follow.[13] However this may be, we must look upon these arguments as a serious attempt to give a rational explanation to the problem of the immortality of the soul. Further, if one admits the theory of ideas, he acknowledges the above arguments as valid, if not conclusive.[14]

b) Immortality in the *Republic*

In the *Republic,* Plato produces a new, straight-forward and persuasive proof of the immortality of the soul which must be regarded as supplementary to the already existing proof in the *Phaedo.* According to this new argument, nothing can be destroyed or perish except by its own specific and peculiar evil or disease, for example, ophtalmia for the eyes, disease for the body in general, mildew for grain.[15]

Now the special evils or vices of the soul are injustice, intemperance, cowardice, ignorance. But these do not destroy the soul at all; far from it, as experience shows, the truth is just the opposite: these evils fill the wicked and unjust man with life, vigour and vitality. But if the particular evil or wickedness of the soul is incapable of diminishing and destroying it,[16] then we may safely conclude that the soul must exist forever and, according to the demands of logical sequence, must be immortal as well.[17]

c) Immortality in the *Phaedrus*

In the Phaedrus, the argument for immortality is stated and represented in a general and dogmatical, so to speak, way and relies on the conception of the soul as self-mover and originator of all movement and consequently of all life.

The self-mover, Plato argues, never leaves its motion, never abandons its own nature. It is the source and origin (beginning) of motion for all other things that are not self-moved. In addition, it is ungenerated, that is, without source or beginning, and indestructible and immortal.

But these same attributes may easily and precisely apply to the essence and the very idea of the soul.[18]

Now if this analogy is correct, namely that which moves itself is nothing else but soul, then an unhurried inference is deduced that soul is ungenerated and immortal.[19]

A parallel conception of the soul, as we have already said, as the self-moved source of all motion, we find also in the tenth Book of the *Laws* and more specifically in *Laws* 894, 895 and 896. However, we must remark with Hackforth that here the "indestructibility of the soul is not explicitly asserted but the conclusions of the *Phaedrus* argument are clearly implied."[20]

d) Immortality in the other dialogues

Apart from the previously mentioned dialogues, one finds little else about the soul's immortality in the other dialogues of Plato. In the *Meno,* for instance, Plato examines the pre-existence and immortality of the soul only with reference to the doctrine of recollection and a priori knowledge,[21] but such an argument, which is completed later in the *Phaedo,* hardly "survives logical scrutiny."[22]

The *Symposium* seems to recognize only the immortality of procreation and the subjective immortality of fame.[23] It does not recognize personal immortality, only a "vicarious survival."[24] As to the *Timaeus,* no serious student of Plato could discover any concrete and solid material concerning the immortality of the soul other than that which has already been noted: 1) the mythical distinction between the immortal part of the soul fashioned by the Demiurge (41D, 69C2) and the mortal parts created by the celestial gods (42D) and 2) the location of the three parts of the soul in certain organs of the body, i.e., the immortal situated in the head, the spirited in the heart and the appetitive in the belly (69D-70E).

Having completed a survey of Plato's views on the immortality of the soul and before turning to the second consideration – the survival of the soul after death – we must generally remark on two points:

1. Whether the immortality of the soul refers to the soul in its entirety or to only its rational part.

2. The precise meaning of *psyche pasa athanatos* (*Phaedrus* 245CB).

Regarding the first point, we may say this. Consistent with what we have earlier said about the soul as simple, uniform and incomposite of itself but in connection with the body as assuming certain phases (spirit, appetite) which are temporary and exist only as long as the soul is connected with the body, we shall conclude that immortality applies to the soul in its entirety, to the wholeness of the soul as a rational and spiritual entity and as a vital principle and acting force.[25]

The second point, the exact meaning of *psyche pasa,* troubled both ancient and modern scholars and is discussed by Frutiger and Hackforth at some length. The former, while he examines the usage of *pas* with and without the article, finally rejects the problem as involving us in pointless difficulty and adopts the distributive meaning, translating *psyche pasa* not into *pasa e psyche* but into "every soul," parallel to its correlative *pan soma.* He concludes ". . . is it not very probable that *psyche pasa* ought to be translated, not in the same fashion as *pasa e psyche* from which it differs grammatically, but conformably to *pan soma* its correlative, that is to say for each soul, no matter which soul?"[26]

Hackforth, on the one hand, argues that there is no distinction here between collective and distributive senses[27] and, on the other hand, prefers the rendering of *psyche pasa athanatos* as "all soul is immortal, because the collective sense is that primarily demanded by the logic of the argument."[28] Further, whereas Hackforth admits that *Phaedrus,* 245C-246A, cannot be regarded as a direct argument or proof for the immortality of individual souls, he is convinced, "that Plato regarded any demonstration of the immortality of 'soul' in general as applicable to individual souls."[29]

The whole question of the individual's immortality has been well stated by Gaye: "So far as personal immortality is concerned, it supplies at most a negative argument; that is to say, it creates a certain presumption in favour of personal immortality in so far as it tends to invalidate the popular view of the finality of death. There is certainly a sense in which the soul survives the death of the individual *empsychon,* but whether this soul continues to exist as a conscious personality is, of course, a different question, and there is nothing in the proof of immortality which we have been considering that can be said to furnish a direct argument in favour of it. . . . From whatever source he may have derived his justification for believing in personal immortality, there can be no doubt that he did believe in it, and moreover that he considered the proof that all soul is immortal to give some support to the belief."[30]

Finally, it might be observed in passing that the myths of *Phaedo,* 107C ff, *Republic* 614 ff, and *Gorgias* 524 ff assume individual immortality.

In conclusion, we must address ourselves to the second consideration – whether Plato has proved that the soul survives death and continues a conscious existence. What kind of inference may be deduced from the above pages? The answer lies in Hackforth's words: "I believe that in both *Republic* X and *Phaedo,* he (Plato) thinks he has proved it; in Phaedo particularly the repeated use of *apodeknynai, logon didonai* and the like . . .taken together with Socrates' emphatic conclusion at 106E *pantos mallon psyche athanaton kai anolethron kai to onti esontai emon ai psychai en Aidou* seems conclusive, despite Socrates' encouragement of 'honest doubt' at 107B. The final argument of *Phaedo* no less than *Phaedrus* appears, however, to regard personal immortality as a corollary of the immortality of 'soul.' "[31]

For Plato the immortality of the soul in general and of the individual in particular was not a pious hope and an "ethical postulate."[32] On the contrary, it was a serious[33] and fundamental problem,[34] which he tried to prove rationally. Further, it was a firm belief, a strong and unshaken conviction, a certainty, a reality. By his very conviction, we are urged to accept his premise.

Thus Plato passionately and firmly believed not broadly in the unseen, in the spiritual, in the ideal, but in the immortality of the soul and more particularly in personal immortality, in self-existence after death, in survival with full consciousness and continued self-identity.

1. *Phaedo* 70B2-4.
2. *Phaedo* 70A-72E.
3. *Phaedo* 72E-76C.
4. *Phaedo* 76E-77A1-5.
5. *Phaedo* 77A6-77D1-6.
6. *Phaedo* 78C, D, E—79A, B.
7. *Phaedo* 84C-102A.
8. *Phaedo* 91C-102A.
9. *Phaedo* 102B-105B4.
10. *Phaedo* 105B5-E.
11. *Phaedo* 106 A-E This additional examination of the indestructibility of the soul has been variously interpreted. J. Burnet, *Plato' Phaedo,* Oxford, 1911, n. on 105E10, holds that the *athanaton* is, ipso facto, *anolethron.* L. Robin, *Phaedo* (Bude'ed, 1949) n. on 106D, remarks, "nonmortal . . . est par definition indestructable"; A. E. Taylor, *Plato,* p. 206, argues as follows: "He is not actually called on to argue this fresh point, since his auditors at once assert their conviction that if what is 'undying' is not imperishable, nothing can be supposed to be so, whereas there are, in fact, imperishables, such as God and 'the for of life.' Thus, in the end, the imperishability of the soul is accepted as a consequence of that standing conviction of all Greek religion, that *to athanaton* = *to theion* = to *aftharton.*" Prof. J. B. Skemp, *The Theory of Motion in Plato's Later Dialogues,* p. 8, calls it a "blatant principii." R. Hackforth, *Plato's Phaedo,* p. 164, sees "at 106D on the surface, no more than a rhetorical flourish which dismisses the question at issue as if it should never have been raised; but it may be that beneath the surface there is an appeal to religious faith if the soul is deathless it is divine . . ." Also see H. Williamson, *The Phaedo of Plato,* edited with introduction and notes, London, MacMillan and Co., Ltd., 1904, pp. 216-217; R. S. Bluck, *Plato's Phaedo,* p. 188; O. O'Brien, "The Last Argument of Plato's Phaedo," *The Classical Quarterly,* n. s. Vols. XVII, no, 2, 1967, pp. 198-231 and XVIII, no. 1, 1968, pp. 95-106. In conclusion, I feel any kind of exegesis of the exact meaning of *athanatos* and *anolethron* of the final proof, either etymological, literal or speculative points to the same interpretation, namely, athanatos = anolethros = athanatos.
12. *Phaedo* 106E9, 107A1, comp. also 106E1-8. It must be noted here that Simmias 107B remains in doubt about the assertions concerning the soul's immortality. To his doubts, Socrates recommends a more through examination of the matter. Socrates' suggestion here does not imply that Plato himself doubted the validity of his previous arguments.
13. Nemesius, *de Nat. Homin.* C. 2, p. 55.
14. *Phaedo* 76E4-9; 77A1-5; G. Rodier, *Les preuves de l'mmortalité d'après 'le Phedon,' Etudes de philosophie Greque,"* Paris, 1957, p. 154, makes somewhat similar comments.

15. *Republic* 609A.
16. *Ibid.*, 609B9-610E10.
17. *Ibid.*, 611A1-2
18. *Phaedrus* 245C5-246A1-2.
19. *Ibid.*, 246A1-2.
20. R. Hackforth, *Plato's Phaedo*, p. 23.
21. *Meno* 80D ff, 81C ff and the inference 86B1-2.
22. R. Hackforth, *Plato's Phaedo*, p. 19.
23. Symposium 207D, 208A7-8, B1-3; 212A6-7.
24. R. Hackforth, *Plato's Phaedo*, p. 20. It must be further noted that Hackforth, "Immortality in Plato's Symposium" in *Classical Review*, LXIV (1950) pp. 35-43, and again in *Plato's Phaedo*, pp. 20-21, maintains that "the Symposium shows us a relapse into temporary scepticism; it drops the claim that soul, collective or individual, is imperishable." See also G. M. A. Grube, *Plato's Thought*, p. 149, note on Symposium 206C, 208C. J. V. Luce, in his reply to Hackforth's "Immortality in Plato's Symposium," *Classical Review*, N. S. II (1952) pp. 137-41 (pp. 135-7) here disagrees with Hackforth, holding that there is no cleavage between *Phaedo* and *Symposium* on the immortality of the soul. He further remarks that the apparent inconsistencies are reconcilable when one remembers that the *Phaedo* emphasizes the immortality of divine soul and the Symposium, the immortality of the human nature. Luce's position is supported by R. S. Bluck, *Plato's Phaedo*, p. 28 n. 1. Prof. H. Cherniss; in a note in *Classical Review*, N. S. III (1953) p. 131, points to *Laws* 712BC, "as by itself proving the invalidity" of Hackforth's conclusion and as alluding to a personal survival. A. E. Taylor, *Plato*, p. 228 n. 1, insists that there is not a single word in Symposium which speaks of the perishability of the soul.
25. R. K. Gaye, *The Platonic Conception of Immortality* pp. 37, 41, refers to Archer-Hind's "On Some Difficulties in the Platonic Psychology," *Journal of Philology*, X (1882) pp. 120-131; especially pp. 129-31; and *Phaedo* (1894) London, pp. XXXII-XXXVII, and concludes that it is as a single nature that the soul is immortal. W. C. K. Guthrie, "Plato's views on the nature of the Soul," *Recherches sur la Tradition Platonicienne, in Entretiens sur l'antiquite classique*, Tome III, p. 19, and J. Adam, *The Republic of Plato*, II, p. 427 n. on 611B12, are of the opinion that soul in its true nature is the highest part, the logisticon and this logisticon alone is perfect, divine and immortal, K. F. Hermann takes up this point in his instructive dissertation: "Praemissa est disputatio de partibus animae immortalibus secundum Platonem," in Index Scholarum, publice et Privatium in Academia Georgia Augusta per semestre hibernum, anni MDCCCL-MDCCCLI A die XV, Octobris usque ad XV Martii, habentarum, Gottingae, pp. 8-9. He claims that Plato intended to represent only the rational part of the soul as immortal and the other two parts as mortal. He is charged by G. Grote, *Plato and the Other Companions of Socrates*, London (1867) II, p. 161 n. a, with failing to realize that Plato sometimes held one language and sometimes another, and that there exists a discrepancy between *Phaedo* and the other Platonic dialogues.
26. C. Frutiger, *Mythes de Platon*, p. 134.
27. R. Hackforth, *Plato's Phaedrus*, p. 64
28. R. Hackforth, *Plato's Phaedrus*, p. 64 n. 3. J. B. Skemp, *The Theory of Motion in Plato's Later Dialogues*, p. 3. n. 1, is in favour of

the collective translation and writes: "pan soma at 245E4 . . . seems the counterpart of psyche pasa here and both seem to have a meaning approximating to pasa e psyche and pan to apsychon at 246B."

29. R. Hackforth, *ibid.*, p. 64-65.

30. R. K. Gaye, *The Platonic Conception of Immortality*, p. 39. A. E. Taylor's view on personal immortality, *Plato*, p. 207, n. is quite convincing and worth quoting: "If the question is asked whether the faith defended in the *Phaedo* is a belief in 'personal' immortality, I can only reply that though the language of philosophers was not to acquire a word for 'personality,' for many centuries, the faith of Socrates is a belief in the immortality of his *psyche* and by his *psyche* he means the seat or suppositum of all we call 'personal character' and nothing else: 'tendence of the soul' is precisely what we call the development of moral personality." G. M. A. Grube, *Plato's Thought*, p. 148 and B. Bosanquet, *A Companion to Plato's Republic*, pp. 406-7, argue that the soul's immortality involves complete loss of personality together with a merger of the rational element with the world soul or cosmic mind. One wonders whether such views do not lead towards a pantheistic interpretation. The following words of R. D. Archer-Hind, *The Phaedo of Plato*, p. XXXII are a refutation of such mistaken views: "Plato knew well that neither he nor anyone else could demonstrate the immortality of individual souls, yet he was strongly disposed to believe . . . that every soul on its separation from the body will not be reabsorbed in the universal, but will survive as a conscious personality even as it existed before its present incarnation."

31. R. Hackforth, *Plato's Phaedrus*, p. 65, n. 1.

32. P. Shorey, *The Unity of Plato's Thought*, p. 40 (or 166).

33. C. Ritter, *The Essence of Plato's Philosophy*, pp. 119, 301. See also the very interesting and illuminating article by the Rt. Hon. Sir P. Duncan, "Immortality of the Soul in Platonic Dialogues and Aristotle," in *Philosophy*, Vol. XVII, 1942, London, pp. 304-323, who endorses and attempts to justify Ritter's conclusion as "irresistible."

34. Important and fundamental, yes, but not to the extent which M. F. Sciacca, "Il problema dell'immortalita dell'anima et metempsicosin Platone," *Studi Sulla fiilosofiia, antica*, Napoli, 1935, p. 221, would have it when he writes that the whole of Plato's philosophy addresses itself to the problem of the immortality of the soul and of the destiny of man: "Dopo cio e'evidente, che attorno al problema dell'immortalita dell'anima eal destino dell'nomo si articola tutta la fiilosofiia di Platone, il cui fondamento come resta confermato eticoreligioso."

AN ASSESSMENT – CONCLUSION

We have considered the views of Plato on the human soul and its immortality and have arrived at some conclusions. In the present chapter we shall bring together these findings and attempt an assessment. Methodological considerations compel us to follow the same pattern-division as in the previous chapters.

The scope of the present chapter requires us to make a few general observations by way of introduction. Plato cannot be regarded as a psychologist in the modern sense of the word. Further, his theory of man (of the human soul) is neither uniform nor consistent. His ideas on the soul are not logically arranged in a single scientific work but are scattered throughout the dialogues. He does not offer a scientific analysis of the human mind, and any attempt to discuss an ordered system of psychology in his dialogues will fail. His main concern is not psychology as a discipline or a science, but man in relation to the universe, to the state, and to society. His primary interest is in politics, ethics, education and in the famous theory of ideas (the basis of his philosophy). In fact, he discusses the problem of the soul and its immortality only in connection with politics, ethics and the theory of ideas. However this may be, Plato has contributed a great deal toward an understanding of man's inner conflict in a rapidly changing modern world. He has also made acute psychological observations which have found their way into psychology, anthropology, philosophy and theology in general.

Having made these general remarks, I must now go on to summarize Plato's views on man or, to be more precise, on the nature of soul.

To begin, Plato's discussion of the human soul and its immortality is clearly distinguished from that of his predecessors. Earlier precursors did not consider the problem of the soul as a separate issue and failed to produce an analytic statement apart from the unclear and often contradictory references found in myth and popular belief. It remained for Plato to initiate the imaginative dialogues which were to explore the intricate problem of the human soul in a logical and dialectical fashion.

Plato views man in dualistic fashion with accent on the superiority of the soul. For him man is a compound structure, consisting of two clearly distinct entities: body, which is mortal, a tool and instrument of the soul, and which in time passes away and soul which is immortal, a senior and permanent entity. Soul and body are treated as separate, distinct, and independent entities belonging to two different worlds.

The body is related to the visible world and belongs to the material and sensible world. It is mortal, subject to corruption and will decay after the moment of physical death. But what is more important is this: While the soul is the reviving force of the body, confining itself in the body during life on earth and likened by Plato to a sailor in a boat or a prisoner in a jail, body, according to Plato, is nothing but a prison-house, a tomb, an encumbrance, a hindrance to the soul. The body acts as a perpetual impediment to the higher activities of the soul and on the whole is the source of evil, disorder and corruption.

The soul, as we have seen, in every way resembles the invisible and belongs to the divine, immaterial and eternal realm. It is a pure spiritual principle, a rational distinct entity, the subject of thought and intelligence, the seat of individual freedom and responsibility; it is the self-mover and the source and first principle of all other things that are moved; it is the source and origin of life the life itself, and as such it is bound to be immortal, divine, indestructible and ungenerated.

With reference to the soul's origin, Plato is of two minds and seems to employ two languages. At times he speaks of the soul as uncreated, ungenerated and absolutely without beginning (*Phaedrus*). At other times he refers to it either as being created by Demiurge (*Timaeus*) or as being produced first, as the first born of all things and prior to the body (*Laws*). These antithetical views, as we have established in the preceding pages, can be resolved by concluding that Plato speaks of the human soul as a created thing; that is, that the individual soul was created by God in time or along with time.

Regarding a division of the soul (the tripartite doctrine), Plato assumes an incomposite, uncompounded and simple soul with, so to speak, mental impulses, spiritual faculties, transitory and temporary manifestations, and modes or phases which owe their existence to the soul's connection with the body and not to the existence of the real and distinct parts or elements.

Speaking of the immortality of the soul (his favorite theme), Plato teaches that the soul as a purely spiritual, rational, simple and indestructible entity will continue in unending and eternal existence, apart from the body. The soul for Plato is inherently and intrinsically immortal, viz, in its own right and in virtue of its nature as soul, by its inherent deathlessness.

Finally, Plato's concern with soul led him to a remarkable view of man. He sees man not as the helpless product of his own impulses (Freud) or a stimulus-response organism (behaviorism). Rather, he views man as a rational, spiritual being, a free and responsible agent, a unique individual, destined for eternity. Further, Plato is concerned with man's dignity, his moral, religious and spiritual development, with his likeness to God.[1] He is also concerned with man's self-awareness and self-realization with the harmonious development of the entire man.[2] As the greatest philosopher, educator and most original thinker of all times, he was interested in the humanization of society. This, he felt, must be the function of education. His own words state his position best: ". . . a sound education . . . will have the greatest tendency to civilize and humanize."[3] He goes on to observe, ". . . man is a tame or civilized animal; nevertheless, he requires proper instruction and a fortunate nature, and then of all animals he becomes the most divine and most civilized; but if he be insufficiently or ill educated he is the most savage of earthly creatures."[4]

1. *Theaet.* 176B1-2; *Rep.* 501A-C1-5; *Laws* 716A-E.

2. The above view that Plato was genuinely interested in man and his well-being has its supporters and critics. The former are: E. Meyer, Geschichte des Altertums, Bd. V. 191, pp. 364-365, 1902; G. E. Burckhardt, Individuum und Allgemeinheit in Platons Politeia, Halle, 1913, p. 15; E. Barker, Greek Political Theory, London, 1960, 26-27; J. Wild, Plato's theory of man, Harvard, 1946, p. 132; R. B. Levinson, In Defense of Plato, Harvard, 1953, p. 524; R. W. Hall, Plato and the Individual, The Hague, 1963. The latter critics argue that Plato was not concerned at all with the individual and his welfare but was indifferent, if not hostile, towards man; U. V. Wilamowitz, Platon, I, Berlin, 1919, pp. 394-395; J. Stenzel, Platon der Erzieher, Leipzig, 1928, p. 138; W. Fite, P. Friedlander, Platon, Vol. II, Berlin, 1954, p. 118; K. R. Popper, The Open Society and its Enemies, Vol. I., The Spell of Plato, London, 1957, pp. 103-104; R. H. S. Crossman, Plato Today, N.Y., 1959; see also H. D, Rankin, Plato and the Individual, N.Y., 1964, pp. 12-13, ns. 1, 2.

3. *Rep.* 416C1-4; trans. B. Jowett, The Dialogues of Plato, vol. II, p. 267.

4. *Laws* 766A1-5; trans. B. Jowett, The Dialogues of Plato, vol. IV, p. 333. cf. Arist. Pol. I, 2.

APPENDIX I

Plato's Theology: Recent Approaches

There is no doubt that Plato's theology, which is closely related to his psychology, is extremely complicated. Part of the difficulty stems from the fact that Plato applies widely, if not sometimes arbitrarily, the term God (Theos) and the adjective Divine (Theios). In the *Timaeus,* for instance, the word God or gods, on the one hand, is used for the Demiurge, for the created Universe (*Tim.* 34B, 92C), for the stars and planets (*Tim.* 40D), for the gods of popular theology (*Tim.* 40E), and for the plurality of good souls in *Laws* X; the adjective Divine is mainly associated with the Forms.[1] However complicated and perplexing, I shall endeavour to make a few general remarks on Plato's theology, especially on the identification of God with the idea of Good, which has caused so much dispute among the Platonic scholars. What follows then is not an exhaustive examination of the entire subject; such a venture would require detailed study of all the Platonic passages and all the available sources and would cover many hundreds of pages. Rather, what is included here is simply a brief survey of recent views of Platonic scholars on the nature of God and the identification of God with the Idea of Good.

Scholars have recently approached the problem of Deity from a natural and ontological point of view. They have supported the opinion that the soul is a source of movement and, consequently, God.[2] Indeed, we do meet such assertions in Plato's dialogues, where he expressly states that "soul is identical with the prime origin and motion of what is, has been and shall be, and of all that is opposite to these, seeing that it has been plainly shown to be the cause of all change and motion in all things . . . it has been proved most sufficiently that the soul is of all things, the oldest, since it is the first principle of motion."[3] And "All soul is immortal . . . and this is also the source and beginning of motion for all other things which have motion."[4]

While some interpreters have been content with the equation of Soul to Deity, the late Prof. Taylor goes further in identifying God with Creator and Best Soul.[5] This identification is characterized by Solmsen as arbitrary.[6]

One may note here that the later Prof. Cornford neither holds such a view as mentioned above, nor regards Demiurge as a religious figure (Deity). Rather he views it as a symbol, a mythical one.[7] Even he finds it difficult to identify the visible Universe with the Demiurge and prefers "to hold back from this or any other conclusion and confine his attention to the world with its body and soul and the reason they contain."[8]

On the other hand, H. Charniss, contrasting and combining various Platonic passages, quite clearly observes that ". . . the work of the Demiurge is the work of Mind (Nous) (*Timaeus* 47E3-4) and Mind can exist only in Soul (46D5-6, 30B3; cf. *Philebus* 30C9-10; *Sophist* 249A), so that the Demiurge must be a soul."[9]

Prof. Grube, on the one hand, identifies the World Soul with the Demiurge.[10] Theiler, on the other, equates the Demiurge "with the Reason in the World Soul."[11] Needless to say, we cannot accept their inferences for the simple reason that in Plato's eyes World Soul is nothing more than a mixture of absolute and corporeal beings.[12]

All of the above-mentioned critics have insisted on the fact that Plato's God was equal to Demiurge or Best Soul, but Prof. Hackforth, on the other hand, takes exactly the opposite view. In a brief but interesting article, he pointed out: (a) that Mind is an ultimate principle, independently existent and an entirely separate entity from the soul, and (b) that "Mind and Mind alone" is identified with God, not the soul or even the Best Soul.[13]

As a matter of fact, Plato speaks quite clearly and emphatically on this issue. He writes that Nous, "intelligence, cannot be present in anything apart from the soul."[14] Further, it cannot exist apart from the soul. "Surely reason and mind could never come into being without soul."[15] In other words, it is explicit that Nous is neither an ultimate principle nor an entity distinct from the soul and identified with God. It is simply, according to Plato, a secondary associate of the Soul, the soul's ability (cf. Republic 508E) to "see the ideas or the state in the soul produced by sight of them."[16] Nous is, as Taylor rightly noted, soul's "vehicle";[17] it is "thinkable as a function of the immortal part of the soul,"[18] an intellectual function. Generally speaking, Hackforth's attempt to establish the Platonic Deity as Nous, attractive as it is, "is perhaps rather too Aristotelian."[19]

It is of great interest to mention Jaeger's attitude towards the Platonic theological problem, although he wrote no single work on this subject as he did on the theology of the early Greek philosophers. Jaeger points out that Plato's "primary approach to the problem was the Socratic and not the pre-Socratic one," that is to say, he approached it from an ethical and moral angle, admitting at the same time the diversity of aspects and forms of the Divine in Plato.[20]

We must now turn our attention to what Plato himself and his commentators have to say about the Idea of Good and whether the following mathematical equation, so to speak, The IDEA OF GOOD = GOD is proved true or not.

Plato's Idea of Good as the source of knowledge and truth makes the Forms intelligible and gives the power of knowing to the mind. Further, the Form of Good is not only the source of knowledge of things, but also of their very being and essence. This does not necessarily imply that the Idea of Good is not the same thing as reality, but the Good is of a still higher essence than all this. In other words, the Good itself is a Form, as any other form, but there is a basic difference between the Idea of

Good and the other Forms: the former is the origin, the cause, of knowledge, truth and reality – the supreme principle of the intelligible word. The latter are its derivatives; that is, the other forms derive their truth, knowledge and being from the Form of Good. All other forms are subordinate to the form of Good.[21,22]

Next we come to consider the vexed question, can God be identified with the Idea of Good or not? Affirmative and negative theories claim the support of distinguished scholars.

Among those interpreters who favor the identification are E. Zeller and J. Adam. Both refer to various passages of Plato's dialogues, and more particularly to *Philebus* 22B 6-10, C 1-3: "I remember a theory . . . about pleasure and intelligence, to the effect that neither of them is the good, but something else, different from either and better than both . . . it couldn't continue to be identical with the good, could it?"[23] They argue strongly that the Demiurge is identical and equivalent to the Idea of Good.[24]

This identification has been challenged by many equally prominent scholars and critics of Plato on the ground that the Idea of Good is not a soul or a personal being at all. On the contrary, it is the supreme form of all the forms and the cause and source of knowledge (science), truth and being.[25] I share the interpretation with some reservations regarding exactly what Plato meant by each term: God-Good.

In view of Plato's reluctance to describe and define exactly his Deity (*Tim.* 28C, *Rep.* 506D-E, *Second Epistle,* 312E, *Seventh Epistle* 341C-D), of the clash of opinions among his scholars and critics, and of this very brief survey, it is a difficult and venturesome task to draw definite conclusions regarding Plato's theology in general. At any rate, I am inclined, with Prof. Dodds, "to explain Plato's lack of clarity on this subject by the cleavage between his mythical or religious thinking and his dialectical or philosophical thinking, and the fact that the former was not bound, or not bound in the same degree as the latter, by the requirement of logical consistency. Our confusion about Plato's God is, I think, an instance. His philosophical thinking about the nature of goodness and the truth led him to posit an Absolute, which is the form of the Good: this Absolute is hardly a possible object of worship, and he nowhere in fact calls it of any of the Forms a God. His religious feeling, on the other hand, created the figure of a benevolent and mighty (though not omnipotent) Father-God, father and maker of God and men and of the world itself. If we try to identify the two, in the hope that they will add up to the equivalent of One Christian Deity we make, as I think, nonsense. . . . I incline to see in him the highest God of Plato's personal faith, whom we meet also at the end of the sixth letter, and whom I should suppose Plato commonly has in mind when he speaks of Theos in the singular without further explanation . . . Plato then, if I am right in my general view, admits two types of belief or two levels of truth, which we may call respectively truths of religion and truths of reason. The former are, as such, indemonstrable, and he does not claim for them more than a probability that this or something like it (*Phaedo*, 114D) is true. I find nothing surprising in this: Most men including, I suspect, most philosophers, believe in practice a good many things which they are incapable of proving. But since Plato preferred to convince his readers by reasoning, if possible, rather than by emotive eloquence, he continually tried to transpose his religious beliefs from the mythical to the philosophical level, thus transforming them into truths of reason."[26]

1. M. Dies, *Author de Platon*, Paris, 1927, II, p. 555; R. C. Hackforth, "Plato's Theism," in the *Classical Quarterly*, 1936, Vol. XXX, p. 4, n. 1.

2. See J. B. Skemp, *The Theory of Motion in Plato's Dialogues*, Cambridge, 1942, p.. 112-115. R. Demos, "Plato's Metaphysics," *Journal of Philosophy*, 1935, XXXII, p. 562, says (*Phaedrus* 245e) ". . . we thus posit a principle of inherent spontaneity, a self-initiating motion, and this is the psyche and ultimately God." See also H. Cherniss, *Aristotle's Criticism* of *Plato and the Academy*, Vol. I, 1944, pp. 606-607 (Appendix XI); and J. Burnet, *Greek Philosophy*, pp. 335-337; J. E. Rexine, *Religion in Plato and Cicero*, Philosophical Library, N.Y., 1968, pp. 28-29. Of particular interest are F. Solmsen, *Plato's Theology*, 1942, p. 113 and E. Frank's review, *American Journal of Philology*, Vol. 4 LXVI, 1945, pp. 92-96.

3. *Laws*, X, 896A7-10, B1-4; trans. R. G. Bury, *Plato, Laws*, London (1926) II, p. 337 in LCL.

4. *Phaedrus* 245C; trans. R. Hackforth, *Plato's Phaedrus*, Cambridge (1952), pp. 63-4.

5. A. E Taylor, *A Commentary on Plato's Timaeus*, Oxford, (1928) pp. 82, also 64, 77 ff; Idem. *Plato, The Laws*, (1960) pp. LIII, LIV, 292; Idem. *Plato the Man and His Work*, London, (1960) pp. 442-45, 490-93; Idem. critical notice on F. Solmsen, Plato's Theology, in Mind, (1943), LII, p. 181. Although Taylor is in favor of this identification, he does not minimize the difficulties of the whole matter (*A Commentary on Plato's Timaeus*, p. 678). F. Solmsen, *Plato's Theology*, p. 121 n. 43, seems to suggest that Bovet and Demos are of the same opinion as Taylor, when he writes: "Bovet (Ch. II, n. 27) looks in Timaeus for confirmation of his theory that the Platonic definition of god would be 'un dieu est ame parfait' (p. 152 f). Demos, on the other hand, *The Philosophy of Plato*, London (1939) pp. 99-125, relies as far as I can see mainly on Timaeus, and fails to do full justice to Laws."

6. F. Solmsen, *Plato's Theology*, p. 113, particularly p. 121 n. 43. R. Hackforth, "Plato's Theism," in *Classical Quarterly* (1936), 30, p. 6, also rejects this idea: ". . . however, whether we believe this or not, it is certainly not the case that Laws X asserts the doctrine of One God, viz., the Best Soul."

7. F. M. Cornford, *Plato's Cosmology*, London, (1937), pp. 34, 35, 37, 38, 197.

8. F. M. Cornford, *Ibid*., p. 39.

9. *Aristotle's Criticism of Plato and the Academy*, Vol. I, Baltimore, 1944, p. 425: ". . . for it is Soul that is the principle of all motion and 'arrangement' and so the artificer of everything whether 'natural' or 'artificial.'" *Laws*, 892A, 896A-D; *Phaedrus*, 245D, 246D, 6-7; op. cit. pp. 251, 603, 605, especially 607. God, therefore, must be "soul having nous," or "enlightened soul." *Laws* 897B; *cf Timaeus* 46 E4.

10. G. M. Grube, *Plato's Thought*, London, 1935, p. 170. See also in

H. Cherniss, op. cit. 603 and F. Solmsen op. cit. p. 121 n. 43. A diversity of approach is found in W. Jaeger's *Paedeia* as well, Vol II, p. 415, 39a, but for that later.

11. W. Theiler, *Zur Geschichte der teleologischen Naturbetrachtung.* p. 72, "als Verdoppelung der Weltseele . . . als Hinausprojektion gleichsam ihrer Kunstlerich wirkenden Seite"; F. M. Cornford, op. cit. p. 197 and H. Cherniss, op. cit. p. 603.

12. *Tim.* 35A.

13. R. C. Hackforth, "Plato's Theism," in *Classical Quarterly,* (1936) 30, p. 7; Idem. *Plato's Phaedrus,* p. 71.

14. *Tim.* 30b3, trans. F. M. Cornford, *Plato's Cosmology,* p. 33.

15. *Philebus* 30 10; also *Soph.* 249A. See also H. Cherniss, *Aristotle's Criticism of Plato and the Academy,* p. 425; J. B. Skemp, *The Theory of Motion in Plato's Later Dialogues,* Cambridge (1942) p. 112.

16. H. Cherniss, *ibid.,* p. 607.

17. A. E. Taylor, critical notice of F. Solmsen, Plato's Theology, in *Mind,* LII (1943) p. 181.

18. J. H. M. M. Loenen, *De Nous in het Systeem Van Plato's Philosophie,* Dissertatie Universiteit van Amsterdam (1951) Jasonpers Universiteitspers, Amsterdam, pp. 55, 56, 57, 58, 269 and 270. This is a very informative and interesting terminological philological and philosophical investigation of the nous-psyche "the development of the teleological explanation of nature and its place in the system"; also R. C. Lodge, "Mind in Platonism," in *Philosophical Review,* 3 (1926) pp. 201-20.

19. J. B. Skemp, op. cit. p. 113 and H. Cherniss op. cit. p. 608.

20. W. Jaeger, Paideia, *The Ideals of Greek Culture,* Oxford, 1944, Vol. 2, p. 415 n. 39b.

21. *Republic* 508E3-509B:

> "Τοῦτο τοίνυν τὸ τὴν ἀλήθειαν παρέχον τοῖς γιγνωσκομένοις καὶ τῷ γιγνώσκοντι τὴν δύναμιν ἀποδιδὸν τὴν τοῦ ἀγαθοῦ ἰδέαν φάθι εἶναι, αἰτίαν δ' ἐπιστήμης οὖσαν καὶ ἀληθείας ὡς γιγνωσκομένης μὲν διανοοῦ, οὕτω δὲ καλῶν ἀμφοτέρων ὄντων, γνώσεώς τε καὶ ἀληθείας, ἄλλο καὶ κάλλιον ἔτι τούτων ἡγούμενος αὐτὸ ὀρθῶς ἡγήσει· . . . . . . Καὶ τοῖς γιγνωσκομένοις τοίνυν μὴ μόνον τὸ γιγνώσκεσθαι φάναι ὑπὸ τοῦ ἀγαθοῦ παρεῖναι, ἀλλὰ καὶ τὸ εἶναί τε καὶ τὴν οὐσίαν ὑπ' ἐκείνου αὐτοῖς προσεῖναι, οὐκ οὐσίας ὄντος τοῦ ἀγαθοῦ, ἀλλ' ἔτι ἐπέκεινα τῆς οὐσίας πρεσβείᾳ καὶ δυνάμει ὑπερέχοντος."

22. While Plato thinks of the Form of the Good so highly others either complain against it as obscure and a source of material for comic poets, Diog. Laert. III 27, in K. Georgoulis, Platonos Politeia Athens (1963), p. 463; v. Goldschmidt, *La Religion de Platon,* Paris (1949) p. 17: "Dèja chez les anciens, l'obscurité du 'bien de Platon' était proverbiale et fournissait une matière a plaisanteries abondamment exploitee par les poetes comiques (n. 1. Diog. Laert., III, 26-27; or they write: "the emptiness of the Platonic Idea or Form of the Good," (K. P. Popper, *The Open Society and Its Enemies, Plato,* Vol. I (1963) (paperback, pp. 274-5 n. 32. See also G. Grote, *Plato and the Other Companions of Socrates,* London (1897) Vol. III, pp. 241-2.

23. Transl. R. Hackforth, *Plato's Examination of Pleasure,* Cambridge, 1945, p. 30.

24. E. Zeller, *Plato and the Older Academy,* New York (1962), pp. 279-92; J. Adam, *The Republic of Plato,* Cambridge (1963) Vol. II, pp. 50-51, 171; and Idem., *The Religious Teachers of Greece,* pp. 442-8 ff. This notion, that the Idea of Good is equivalent to God, is supported also by many others, with variations, of course, such as B. Jowett, *The Works of Plato,* N.Y. p. 128; E. Frank's review of F. Solmsen, "Plato's Theology" in *American Journal of Philology,* Vol. LXVI (1945) pp. 93-6; P. Frutiger, *Les Mythes de Platon,* Paris (1930) pp. 206-7; R. Muguier, *Les Sens du Mot Theios chez Platon,* Paris, (1930) pp. 130-32; W. F. R. Hardie, *A Study in Plato,* Oxford (1936) pp. 155-6; R. L. Nettleship, *Lectures on the Republic of Plato,* London (1963) pp. 232-3; R. C. Lodge, *Plato's Theory of Ethics* (1928) pp. 171, 466 and 502 n. 14; W. Jaeger, Paideia. *The Ideals of Greek Culture,* Vol. II, Oxford (1944) pp. 285 ff and 414-6 n. 39b, 40, 44; E. Hoffmann, *Die griechische Philosophie bis Platon* (1951) Heidelberg, pp. 162 and 175; L. Robin, *Platon,* Paris, (1935) pp. 248-52; M. Dies, *Autour de Platon,* pp. 550-1, 553-5; A. J. Festugiere, *Contemplation et vie contemplative selon Platon,* Paris (1950) pp. 204-5, 265-6; Victor Goldschmidt, *La Religion de Platon,* Paris (1949) pp. 17-62, where he believes that he has been able to presuppose throughout his thesis (and especially pp. 17-62) what Mgr. Dies, Festugiere, M. Moreau and Jaeger interpret in different ways: "Depuis, les travaux de Mgr. Dies, du R. P. Festugiere, de M. Moreau, de M. Jaeger, l'ont renforcee (tout en l'interpretant dans des sens differents) et nous avons cru pouvoir la supposer tout au long notre expose"; W. Temple, *Plato and Christianity,* London (1916) pp. 28-30; U. von Wilamowitz-Moellendorff, *Platon,* Berlin (1919) pp. 633, 685; K. F. Doherty, *God and the Good in Plato, the New Scholasticism,* 1956 pp. 459-60, where one finds references in other scholars. We need hardly mention here that determined effort was made in ancient times (Cp. Philo, De Op. Mund. IV 19; Albinus, Epit. IX i, 3; Plutarch, Epit. 1, 3; Stobaeus Ecl. 1, 10, 16; Galen *Hist. Phil.* 25; Hippolytus, Ref. Omn. Haer. I, 19; Theodoret, *Graec. Affect. Cup.* IV, 49, etc.) and in recent years (Jackson, "Plato's Later Theory of Ideas," *J. P.* II, 324; Ritter, Die Kerngedanken der Platonischen Philosophie, 321; Archer-Hind, *Commentary on Timaeus,* p. 95 n. 10 all qtd. by A. N. Rich, "The Platonic Ideas as the thoughts of God," in *Mnemosyne,* Biblioteca Classica batara, Series IV, Vol. VII, Lugduni (1954) p. 132 n. 2, 4., to make the idea dependent upon God as a thought resident in his mind. It will take us too far to point out quite the opposite. Nonetheless, the following

words of A. N. M. Rich, *ibid.*, p. 123 ns. 2.4 are to a great extent a disavowal. "To disprove it is, however, a comparatively simple matter, for reference to the Platonic Dialogue makes it immediately clear that any concrete evidence in favour of this interpretation is completely lacking. Plato never describes the Ideas either as the thoughts of God or as the content of God's mind."

25. Chief supporters of this theory, each with his own way of interpreting, are: J. Burnet, *Greek Philosophy*, pp. 336-7; P. Shorey, *What Plato Said*, Chicago (1933) p. 231; Idem. *Republic of Plato*, pp. 102 n. a; Idem. "The Idea of Good in Plato's Republic," Univ. of Chicago, *Studies in Classical Philology* (1895) p. 239. Shorey, in his criticism, is rather unjustifiable; see ibid. pp. 26-7 n. 4; A. E. Taylor, *Plato, the Man and His Work*, pp. 232 and 288; P. E. Moore, *The Religion of Plato* (1921) Princeton, pp. 312 ff; G. M. A. Grube, *Plato's Thought*, London (1935) pp. 168-9; R. Demos, *The Philosophy of Plato*, London (1939) p. 123; J. B. Skemp, op. cit. p. 115; F. Solmsen, op. cit. pp. 72, 92 and more emphatically in 192 and 195 n. 49; H. Cherniss, pp. 604, 606; E. Gilson, *God and Philosophy*, Yale U. (1959) pp. 26-28; G. C. Field, *The Philosophy of Plato*, London (1949) p. 61; D. Ross, *Plato's Theory of Ideas*, Oxford (1951) pp. 43-44; F. Copleston, *A History of Philosophy*, London (1961) pp. 191 ff; A. H. Armstrong, *An Introduction to Ancient Philosophy*, London (1959) p. 39; J. A. Stewart, *Plato's Doctrine of Ideas*, Oxford (1909) p. 59; H. Reader, *Platon's Philosophische Entwickelung*, Leipzig (1905) pp. 381-2. In addition to these references, one may find others in the brief but interesting article by K. F. Doherty, *God and the Good in Plato*, The New Scholasticism XXX (1956) pp. 441 ff.

26. E. R. Dodds, "Plato and the Irrational," *Journal of Hellenic Studies* (1945) pp. 23, 24; Idem. *The Greeks and the Irrational*, Berkeley and Los Angeles (1963) pp. 221 and 232 n. 67. I quote his words in full because of their importance and because they hardly admit of summary. See also similar notions: J. A. Stewart, *Plato's Doctrine of Ideas*, Oxford (1909) pp. 101-2; K. F. Doherty, "God and the Good" in the *New Scholasticism*, pp. 459-60. It is, however, worth mentioning that A. E. Taylor, *Plato, the Man and His Work*, p. 289, speaks about "Good—Christian God . . . ans realissimum," while Ernst Hoffmann, *Griechische Philosophie bis Platon*, Heidelberg (1951) p. 175, is neither prepared to identify nor to reject it. He nevertheless remarks that Plato, as a philosopher, never gives a result in his Dialogues, but always shows a way which will lead to a result. ". . . Was Platon in seinen Dialogen als Philosophie gibt, ist niemals ein resultat sondern ist immer ein Weg, der zum Resultat, hinfuhren will. . . ."

APPENDIX II

A Comparison of Plato's Tripartite Theory of the Soul to Freud's Structure of Personality

There are some similarities and differences between Freud's tripartite division of the psyche and Plato's with reference to the nature of the human mind and its function. One clear-cut difference is this: Plato looks upon the human soul as a spiritual, rational, and immortal entity. Such a view is absent in the Freudian writings. Freud was the spiritual child of his time; consequently, his theory on man was thoroughly mechanistic and wholly materialistic. Man, to him, is but the creature of the blind and irrational instincts. However this may be, there are some similarities between the two theories with regard to the function of the human mind:

a) Id and Appetite

The id in Freudian terminology corresponds to the irrational appetite, and is regarded by Freud as the basic and most important aspect of the human personality. Further, the id is amoral and blindly anti-social. It knows no right or wrong; it has no consideration for others. It is, in Freud's words: "a chaos, a cauldron, full of seething excitations."[1] Its irrational impulses strive for discharge or satisfaction. The id is governed only by the principle of pleasure.[2]

Plato speaks of the appetite element and Freud of the id as the sources of all of our instincts, drives and desires – of hunger, thirst, love and sex.[3]

Freud's notion that the id is amoral, irrational and antisocial and that it follows the pleasure principle reminds us of Plato's statement that the appetite is "closely connected with pleasure and satisfaction"[4] and that pleasure and pain rule one's soul instead of law and the principles accepted by the society.[5]

Other similarities between id and appetitive element are the following:

Plato refers to the desires as "terrible, savage and irregular"[6] and Freud describes the id as "a chaos, a cauldron full of seething excitations."[7]

Both say that desire and id are dominant, "more extensive, more imposing and more obscure" than reason and ego.[8]

Finally, Freud writes that "the logical laws of thought do not apply in the id, and this is true above all of the law of contradiction. Contrary impulses exist side by side, without cancelling each other. . . ."[9] Plato says the same thing when he writes that because of different desires and impulses "soul is variable and unstable and full of internal conflicts."[10]

b) Ego and Reason

The Freudian ego is similar to the rational element in the Platonic division.[11] The ego, according to Freud, is the rational, conscious aspect of the human personality, which serves to mediate between the id and the external world, between the id and superego.

In mediating between the demands of the id and the pressure of the external world of the environment, the role of the ego here might be compared to that of a chief executive.[12]

Reason, by its very nature, unlike the other two faculties of mind — desire and spirit — should always reflect, examine, and be in control of the other two elements of the soul.[13] The blind and unconscious drives of the id press for satisfaction, the ego modifies or channels these instincts or impulses. However, it should be observed that Freud does not consider the ego to be independent of the id; on the contrary, it is part of the id and derives its power and energy from it. Further, like reason, the ego is guided by the reality principle.[14]

It is interesting to note that Freud makes use of the metaphors of the *Phaedrus* myth and compares the ego to a rider and the id to a horse. Here are his own words: "The ego's relation to the id might be compared with that of a rider to his horse. The horse supplies the locomotive energy, while the rider has the privilege of deciding on the goal and of guiding the powerful animal's movement."[15]

Finally, it must be noted that there is a difference between reason and ego. Reason,[16] as has already been noted, is the master of the other two elements of the soul; ego is the servant of the other two components of personality – id and superego – as well as subject to the forces of the external world.[17]

c) Superego and Spirit

There remains the comparison between the superego and spirited element. The superego is equivalent in many respects to what is traditionally called "conscience," representing internalized prohibitions and restrictions based on the moral standards of parents and, more generally speaking, the values, traditions, and ideals of the society at large. The superego, then, embodies the moral, judicial and idealizing aspect of personality. "The main functions of the superego are (1) to inhibit the impulses of the id, particularly those of a sexual or aggressive nature, since these are the impulses whose expression is most highly condemned by society, (2) to persuade the ego to substitute moralistic goals for realistic ones, and (3) to strive for perfection. That is, the superego is inclined to oppose both the id and the ego, and to make the world over into its own image" (Hall-Lindzey, *Theories of Personality* p. 35).

The functions of the superego are similar to those of the spirited or emotional aspect of the soul. As the superego resists the id,[18] as it criticizes and humiliates the ego,[19] and strives for moral perfection,[20] so the emotional element opposes and fights desire, rebukes the reason and, generally speaking, fights for what it thinks is right and ideal till death and victory.[21]

Further the superego is partly conscious and partly unconscious[22] and irrational, like its Platonic counterpart, the spirited element.[23]

In addition to these similarities there are differences between superego and the spirited element. While the superego, according to Freud, is the "heir" or successor of the Oedipus complex[24] the spirited part, according to Plato, begins at the time of birth.[25] Another difference, as has been discussed earlier, is that while reason dominates the spirit and the desire,[26] superego opposes and is the master of the other two components of human personality: id and ego.[27]

It should be noted here that Freud, like Plato, did not regard these three components of personality[28] as distinct and real entities, continually at war within us. Rather, he used these concepts to express three different aspects of the same person. Hall and Lindzey have pointed out (p. 35, 1970[2]) that "the id, ego, and superego are not to be thought of as manikins which operate the personality. They are merely names for various psychological processes which obey different system principles. Under circumstances these different principles do not collide with one another nor do they work at cross purposes. On the contrary, they work together as a team under the administrative leadership of the ego. The personality normally functions as a whole rather than as three separate segments. In a very general way, the id may be thought of as the biological component of personality, the ego as the psychological component and the superego as the social component."

Prof. Skinner, in his famous book *Science of Human Behavior* (1966, p. 375), finds Freud's description of the mental apparatus quite fictitious.

This is not the place to discuss the virtues and faults of psychoanalysis, but perhaps, in passing, we may say that psychologists, psychiatrists, sociologists, anthropologists, philosophers, theologians and other thinkers are highly critical of Freudian theories on various grounds. The critique of Prof. H. J. Eysenck, a well-known psychologist in the field of personality, may be taken as representative. He observes that psychoanalysis and the theories associated with it are not science, but myth; adherence to them, he goes on to say, is based on emotion and prejudice rather than on fact and reason (in *Uses and Abuses of Psychology,* Penguin Books, 1958, 221-241; esp. pp. 235-241).

Along these same lines of criticism, Marx and Hillix, *Systems and Theories in Psychology,* p. 236, note that "psychoanalysis is more an art, a philosophy, and a practice than a science. The theory is loose and nebulous, sometimes even self-contradictory." Hall and Lindzey, *Theories of Personality,* p. 72 add ". . . Freud may not have been a rigorous scientist nor a first rate theoretician, but he was a patient, meticulous, penetrating observer and a tenacious, disciplined, courageous, original thinker."

In spite of the fact that many critics reject Freudian theory, they agree almost unanimously that Freud exerted a profound and direct influence on psychiatry and clinical psychology. To be specific, the following psychoanalytic concepts entered academic psychology through the work of Sigmund Freud:

1) The unconscious, especially the goal-directed unconscious.

2) Motivation.

3) The significance of early experience.

4) Ego psychology, primary and secondary processes, the structural aspect of personality, and the defense mechanism, particularly repression (D. Shakow, "Psychoanalysis," in D. L. Krantz, ed., *Schools of Psychology,* A symposium of papers, ACC, N. Y., 1969, pp. 110-115; and elsewhere).

1. S. Freud, The Standard Edition of the Complete Psychological Works of S. Freud, trans. and ed. by J. S. Strachey, London, The Hogarth Press, the Institute of Psychoanalysis, 1959, XX, 73.
2. Freud, XX, 74.
3. *Republic* 436A-437E; 439D6-8; 580DE-581; *Philebus* 35D1-3; S. Freud, XX 200; XXII 73.
4. *Republic* 439D6-8 cf *Phaedrus* 246A5-B4; 253-254E.
5. *Ibid.*, 607A.
6. *Phaedrus* 253-254E.
7. Freud XXII, 73.
8. *Republic* 442C, 580E, 588D, Freud XX 195.
9. Freud XXII, 73.
10. *Republic* 611B1-3 trans. by H. D. P. Lee, p. 390. See also *ibid.*, 560A-561E; 587A-C.
11. Freud XXII 76, XVIII 109; Plato, *Republic* 439D5.
12. Freud XX 201.
13. *Republic* 435A-445E; 580D-581E; *Phaedrus* 246A-B; 253A-254E.
14. Freud XX 194; Plato *Republic* 585C ff.
15. XXII 77 cf. XVII. 57; VII. 136.
16. Plato, *Republic* 441E-442E; *Phaedrus* 246A-B; 253A-254E.
17. Freud, XXII 77-78.
18. *Ibid.*, XXII 60-62, 77-78, 109, 243.
19. *Ibid.*, XXII 60, 65, 66.
20. *Freud,* XXII, 65 and 66.
21. Plato, *Republic* 439DE—441AB; *Phaedrus* 246AB and 253A-254E.
22. Freud, XXII 69-71; 75, 78-79.
23. *Rep.* 440B-443E.
24. *Freud,* XXII, 64, 66-67, 79, 129.
25. Plato, *Republic* 441A7-10-441B1-3.
26. Rep. 441E-442E; *Phaedrus* 246A-B and 253A-254E.
27. Freud, XXII, 77-78.

For further insight into the comparison between Plato's tripartite theory of soul and Freud's structure of personality, see: H. J. Eysenck, *Sense and Nonsense in Psychology,* Penguin Books, Md., 1966, p. 153-154; A. R. White, *The Philosophy of Mind,* Random House, N.Y., 1968, pp. 28 and 39-40; A. J. P. Kenny, "Mental Health in Plato's Republic," *Proceedings of British Academy LV,* 1969, pp. 238-241; D. B. Klein, *A History of Scientific Psychology,* Basic Books, Inc., Publishers, N.Y./London, 1970, pp. 47-58; J. E. McKeown, "Sociological misinterpretations of Plato's Republic," American Catholic Sociological Review, XVI, October, 1955, p. 16; W. Ebenstein, Great Political Thinkers, Plato the Present, Holt, Rinehart and Winston, Inc., N. Y., 1969, p. 11-12.

28. For more on Freud's theory of the structure of personality, see the following: Freud, S: *The Ego and the Id,* standard edition, vol. 19, pp. 3-66; *The Unconscious,* standard ed., vol. 14, pp. 159-209; *New Introductory Lectures on Psychoanalysis,* standard edition, vol. 22, ch. 31, pp.

57-80; *An Outline of Psychoanalysis,* standard ed. Vol. 23, pp. 141-207; *The Interpretation of Dreams,* standard ed. Vol. 5, second part, ch. 7. pp. 507-621; *Instincts and their Vicissitudes,* standard ed., Vol. 14, pp. 111-140.

See also: Brenner, C., *An Elementary Textbook of Psychoanalysis,* Doubleday Anchor Books, N.Y., 1957, pp. 33-141; Chaplin, J. P., *Systems and Theories of Psychology,* N.Y., 1965, pp. 410-416; Fine R., *Freud: A Critical Re-Evaluation of His Theories,* N.Y., 1964 (paperback), pp. 82-115; Hall, S. C. and G. Lindzey, *Theories of Personality,* N.Y., 1970, pp. 29-72; Hendrick, I., *Facts and Theories of Psychoanalysis,* Laurel edition, 1966, pp. 155-182, esp. 158-166; Marx, M. and Hillix, W. A., *Systems* and *Theories in Psychology,* N.Y., 1963, pp. 209-214; Mullahy, P., *Oedipus: Myth and Complex: a review of psychoanalysis theory,* Grove Press, N.Y., 1957, pp. 6-8, 36-43; Munroe, L. R., *Schools of Psychoanalytic Thought,* The Dryden Press, 1956, pp. 82-115; Strupp, H. H., *An Introduction to Freud and Modern Psychoanalysis,* Barrow's Educational Series, N.Y., 1967, pp. 12-20; Thompson, C., *Psychoanalysis: Evolution and Development,* Grove Press, N.Y., 1957, pp. 59-77; Wolman, B. B., *Contemporary Theories and Systems in Psychology,* Harper and Row, N.Y., 1960, pp. 241-282; Wolman, B. B., *The Unconscious Mind: the meaning of Freudian psychology,* Prentice-Hall, N.J., (paperback), 1968, pp. 42-65; Zilboorg, G., *Sigmund Freud, his exploration of the mind of man,* N.Y., Norton, 1941; Hall, S. C. A., Primer of Freudian psychology, (Mentor book), 1954, pp. 22-48; esp. 22-35.

APPENDIX III

Plato, Behaviorists and Humanistic Psychologists on Man

While Plato, as it has been noted, views man as a rational, spiritual being, a free and responsible agent destined for eternity, J. B. Watson, the founder of behaviorism, and B. F. Skinner, "the most influential and controversial psychologist of our time" and the main exponent of contemporary behaviorism, look at man in a mechanistic and wholly materialistic way. Man for them is but an animal, just a complex, organic machine.

"Mentalistic" concepts such as soul, mind, consciousness or "subjective terms" such as sensation, perception, image, desire, purpose, are concepts of the past, hangovers from the prescientific times and rejected. As such, they are completely ignored by psychology, which studies "behavior" rather than "unconsciousness." As a science, psychology strives to base its conclusions on objective and experimental data and not on introspection. Soul or mind, therefore, do not exist. What does exist is the body itself. Mental phenomena are reduced to mere states or appearances of the body. Mind or soul is merely the function or the by-product of the brain.[1]

Not all contemporary psychologists, Behaviorists or non-Behaviorists, subscribe to the "radical or metaphysical behaviorism." The mind-body problem, (Watson's "metaphysical point"), "is neither accepted nor rejected for scientific purposes, but simply is considered irrelevant. There seems to be no evidence that a mind-body problem position has a marked influence on the work done by a psychologist. Rather, the scientist seems more likely to accept a mind-body position which harmonizes with his work."[2] Professor Hebb states the case better when he says: "There are two theories of mind, speaking very generally. One is animistic, a theory that the body is inhabited by an entity – the mind or soul – that is quite different from it, having nothing in common with bodily processes. The second theory is physiological or mechanistic; it assumes that mind is a bodily process, an activity of the brain. Modern psychology works with this latter theory only. Both are intellectually respectable (that is, each has support from highly intelligent people, including scientists), and there is certainly no decisive means available of proving one to be right, the other wrong."[3] The relationship between mind-body and the issue of consciousness are debated among philosophers, psychologists and biologists. A great number of psychologists believe that present day psychology should study and examine carefully the conscious phenomena.[4]

In recent years a psychological movement under the name "Third Force" has made its appearance as a strong reaction against the other two forces; against psychoanalysis, which views man as an irrational being, and against behaviorism, which portrays man as a complex, organic machine.[5] The designation "Third Force," generally speaking, incorporates humanistic psychology as well as phenomenological and existential psychology.

Humanistic psychology is concerned with the wholeness and entirety of man, with the dignity of man, and with the uniqueness of the human species. It sees man as a dynamic, conscious, striving, purposeful, and creative organism.[6] The portrayal of man according to the humanistic movement bears many striking similarities with Plato's portrait of man.

1. For further elaboration on how behaviorists view mind, consciousness and other related topics, see the following:

J. B. Watson, *Psychology as a Behaviorist Views* It, Psych. Rev. 20, 1913, pp. 112, 158-177.

———, *Behavior: An Introduction to Comparative Psychology,* N. Y., Holt, Rinehart, Winston, Inc., 1914, pp. 112, 122, 126, 129; 133.

———, *Behaviorism,* rev. ed., University of Chicago Press, Chicago, 1966, pp. 118, 123, 126, 127, 227.

B. F. Skinner, *The Behavior of Organism: An Experimental Analysis,* N.Y., Appleton-Century-Crofts, 1938.

———, *Science and Human Behavior,* N.Y., MacMillan, 1953, pp. 29-42, 45-58, 283-294.

———, *Beyond Freedom and Dignity* (paperback), Bantan-Vintage Books, N.Y., 1972, pp. 175-206.

———, *Walden Two* (paperback), MacMillan, 1972.

R. S. Woodsworth and M. R. Sheenan, *Contemporary Schools of Psychology,* The Ronald Press, Co., N.Y., 1964, pp. 111-129, 162-169.

M. H. Marx and W. A. Hillix, *Systems and Theories in Psychology,* McGraw Hill Book Co., N.Y., 1963, pp. 129-170, 256-262.

B. B. Wolman, *Contemporary Theories and Systems in Psychology,* Harper and Row, Publ., N.Y., 1960, pp. 76-85, 125-139.

R. I. Watson, *The Great Psychologists: from Aristotle to Freud,* J. B. Lippincott Co., N.Y., 1963, pp. 375-76, 385-402.

H. Missiak and V. S. Sexton, *History of Psychology: an Overview,* Grune, Stratton, N.Y., 1966, pp. 328-346.

M. L. Hutt, R. L. Issacson and M. L. Blum, *Psychology, The Science of Interpersonal Behavior,* Harper & Row, N.Y., 1954, pp. 388-392.

J. P. Chaplin and T. S. Krowiec, *Systems and Theories of Psychology,* Holt, Rinehart, Winston, Inc., 1968, pp. 50-55, 257-272.

Th. Dobzshansky, *The Biology of Ultimate Concern,* N.Y., 1967, pp. 64-66.

2. M. H. Marx and W. A. Hillix, *Systems and Theories in Psychology,* McGraw-Hill Book Co., N.Y., 1963, p. 169.

3. *A Textbook of Psychology,* W. G. Saunders Co., Philadelphia, 1961, p. 3.

4. H. Missiak and V. S. Sexton, *History of Psychology: an Overview,* Grune, Stratton, N.Y., 1966, pp. 343-346; Th. Dobzhansky, *The Biology of Ultimate Concern,* pp. 64-67.

5. See also J. S. Wiggins, K. E. Renner, G. L. Clore, R. J. Rose, *The Psychology of Personality,* Addison-Wesley Publ. Co., Reading, Mass., 1971, p. 542-543. "Self-theory is a reaction against the appplication to people of the methods of inquiry developed for physical objects which treat the human psyche as mechanical and chemical processes. It is a reaction against an 'empty black box' approach to man . . . Self-theory is a reaction against the past 70 years of Behaviorism."

6. R. L. Issacson, et al., *Psychology, The Science of Interpersonal* Behavior, Harper & Row, Publ., N.Y., 1965, pp. 392-393.

For more about Humanistic Psychology see the following: F. T. Severin, *Humanistic Viewpoints in Psychology: a Book of Readings,* McGraw-Hill Book Co., N.Y., 1965; F. G. Goble, *The Third Force: the Psychology of Abraham Maslow,* Grossman Publishers, N.Y., 1970; C. Buhler and Melanie Allen, *Introduction to Humanistic Psychology,* Books/Cole Publ. Co., Monterey, California, 1972; J. Stein, *Effective Personality: A Humanistic Approach,* Brooks/Cole Publ. Co., Belmont, California, 1972; J. F. T. Bugental, Challenges of Humanistic Psychology, McGraw Book Co., N.Y., 1967.

BIBLIOGRAPHY

1. *PRIMARY SOURCES*

Greek text: Platonis Opera, ed. by J. Burnet, Vols. 1-5, 1958, Oxford: Clarendon Press.

English translations: The Dialogues of Plato, 4 vols., tr. by B. Jowett, Oxford: Clarendon Press, 1953: Loeb Classical Library and individual dialogues tr. by Cornford, Hackforth, Lee, Taylor, etc.

2. *SECONDARY SOURCES*

Adam, J.—*The Religious Teachers of Greece*, T. T. Clark, Edinburgh, 1923.

—*The Republic of Plato,* ed. with critical notes, commentary, and appendices, Cambridge, Cam. Univ. Press, 1902; 2nd edition with a new introduction by D. A. Rees, 1963, Vols. 1-2.

Alsberg, P.—*In Quest of Man*: a biological approach to the problem of man's place in nature, Pergamon Press, Oxford, 1970.

Archer-Hind, R. D.—*On Some difficulties in the Platonic Psychology,* Journal of Philology, 10, 1882, 120-131.

—*The Phaedo of Plato,* ed. with introduction, notes and appendices, Macmillan, London 1894.[2]

Aristotelis.—*Metaphysica,* Scriptorum Classicorum Bibl. Oxoniensis, by W. Jaeger, 1960.

—*Ethica Nicomachea,* ed. by I. Bywater, Scrip. Class. Biblioth., Oxoniensis, 1949.

—*de Anima.*—Scriptorum Classicorum Bibl. Oxoniensis, ed. by D. Ross, 1959.

Armstrong, A. M. –*An Introduction to Ancient Philosophy,* Methuen, London 1959.[3]

Ballard, E. G.–*Plato's movement from ethics of the individual to a Science of Particulars,* Tulane Studies in Philosophy, Vol. 6 (Studies in Ethics), Tulane University, New Orleans, 1957, 14-60.

Bates, M.–*Man in Nature,* in Foundations of Modern Biology series, Prentice-Hall Inc. 1964.[2]

Bosanquet, B.–*A Companion to Plato's Republic for English Readers,* Rivingtons, London, 1925.[2]

Brandom, F. G. S.–*Man and his Destiny in the Great Religions,* Manchester, 1962.

Brenner, C.–*An Elementary Textbook of Psychoanalysis,* Doubleday Anchor Books, N.Y., 1957.

Buhler, C. and Melanie Allen.–*Introduction of Humanistic Psychology,* Brooks/Cole Publ. Co., Monterey, Ca., 1972.

Burnet, J.–*Early Greek Philosophy,* London, 1930.

–*The Ethics of Aristotle,* ed. with an introduction and notes, London, 1900.

–*Greek Philosophy*: Thales to Plato, MacMillan, London, 1914.

–*Philosophy in The Legacy of Greece,* ed. by Sir. R. Livingstone, Oxford, at the Clar. Press, 57-95.

–*Plato's Phaedo,* ed. with introduction and notes, Oxford at the Clarendon Press, 1959.

–*The Socratic Doctrine of the Soul,* and address, London, 1929.

–*Soul,* in Encyclopaedia of Religion and Ethics, 11, 1920, T. T. Clark, Edinburgh, 737-742.

Cappelle, W.–*Body,* in Encyclopaedia of Religion and Ethics, Vol. 2, 1909, 768-772.

Chaplin, J. P. and T. S. Krowiec–*Systems and Theories of Psychology,* Holt, Rinehart, Winston, Inc., 1968.[2]

Cherniss, H.–*Aristotle's Criticism of Plato and the Academy,* Vol. 1, Baltimore, 1944.

—*Aristotle's Criticism of Pre-Socratic Philosophy*, The Johns Hopkins Press, Baltimore, 1935.

Classen, G. J.—*Sprachilche deutung als triebkraft Platonischen und Sokratischen Philosophierens,* Munchen, 1959.

Copleston, F.—*A History of Philosophy,* Vol. 1: Greece and Rome, Burns & Oates, London, 1961.

Cornford, F. M.—*The Division of the Soul,* The Hibbert Journal, 28, 1929-30, 206-219.

—*The Doctrine of Eros,* The Unwritten Philosophy, Cambridge, 1950.

—*From Religion to Philosophy* (paperback), Harper, N.Y., 1957.

—*Greek Religious Thought,* Dent, London, 1950.

—*Mysticism and Science in the Pythag. Tradition,* The Classical Quarterly, Vol. 16, 1922, 137-150, and 1923, 1-12.

—*Mystery Religions and pre-Socratic Philosophy,* The Cambridge Ancient History, Chapt. 15, 522-577, Vol. 4, 1926.

—*Plato's Cosmology;* The Timaeus of Plato translated with a running commentary, Routledge & Kegan Paul Ltd., London, 1956.

—*The Republic of Plato,* translated with introduction and notes, Oxford at the Clarendon Press, 1961.

Cross, R. C. and A. D. Woozley.—*Plato's Republic: A Philosophical Commentary,* MacMillan, London, 1964.

Cunliff, R. J.—*A Lexikon of the Homeric Dialect,* Blackie, Glasgow, 1924.

de Haan, Bierens.—*Animal Psychology,* Hutchinson, London, 1946.

Demos, R.—*Plato's Metaphysics,* Journal of Philosophy, 32, 1935, 561-578.

—*The Philosophy of Plato,* Scribners, London, 1939.

Diels, H. and W. Kranz.—*Die Fragmente der Vorsokratiker* (Greek and German), 6th ed., 3 Vols., Berlin, 1951-1952.

Dies, M.—*Autour de Platon,* Vol. 2, Beauchesne, Paris, 1927.

Dobzhansky, T.—*The Biology of Ultimate Concern,* Meridian Book World Publi., N.Y., 1971.

—*Mankind Evolving: The Evolution of the Human Species*, New Haven, Yale University Press, 1966.

Dodds, E. R.—*The Greeks and the Irrational,* University of California Press, Berkeley, 1951.

—*Plato and the Irrational,* The Journal of Hellenic Studies, (LXV) 65, 1945, 16-26.

Doherty, K. F.—*God and the Good in Plato,* in New Scholasticism, 30, 1956, 441-460.

Duncan, Sir P.—*Immortality of the Soul in Platonic Dialogues and Aristotle, Philosophy,* 17, 1942, 304-323.

Ehnmark, E.—*Socrates and the Immortality of the Soul,* Eranos, 44, 1946, 105-122.

Eysenck, H. J.—*Sense and Nonsense in Psychology,* Penguin Books, Baltimore, Md., 1966.

Festugiere, A. J.—*Contemplation et vie contemplative selon Platon,* J. Vrin, Paris, 1950.[2]

Fillous, J.—*The Psychology of Animals,* trans. by J. J. Walling, Walker and Co., N.Y., 1963.

Fine, R.—*Freud: a critical re-evaluation of his theories,* N.Y., 1964 (paperback).

Forbes, J. J.—*Socrates,* T. T. Clark, Edinburgh, 1905.

Freeman, K.—*Pre-Socratic Philosophers.* A companion to Diels' Fragmente der Versokratiker, Oxford, 1946.

Freud, S.—*The Interpretation of Dreams,* standard ed. Vol. 14.

—*The Unconscious,* standard ed., Vol. 14.

—*The Ego and the Id,* standard edition, Vol. 19.

—*New Introductory Lectures on Psychoanalysis,* standard edition, Vol. 22, chpt. 31.

—*An Outline of Psychoanalysis,* standard ed., Vol. 23.

Frutiger, P.—*Les Mythes de Platon,* Alcan, Paris, 1930.

Gaus, H.—*Philosophischer Hand Kommentar Zu den Dialogen Platos,* Bern, 1952, I/1.

Gaye, R. K.—*The Platonic Conception of Immortality and its Connection with the Theory of Ideas,* Cambridge Univ. Press, 1904.

Gilson, E.—*God and Philosophy,* Yale University Press, 1941; paperback, 1959.

Goble, F. G.–*The Third Force: the psychology of Abraham Maslow,* Grossman Publishers, N.Y., 1970.

Goldschmidt, V.–*La Religion de Platon,* Paris, 1949.

Gomperz, T.–*The Greek Thinkers,* A History of Ancient Philosophy, trans. by L. Magnus, Vol. I Murray, London, 1901; paperback, 1964.

Grote, G.–*Plato and the other Companions of Socrates,* Vol. 3, J. Murray, London, 1867.

Grube, G. M. A.–*Plato's Thought, Methuen,* London, 1935.
–*The Composition of the World-Soul in Timaeus* 35A-B, Classical Philology, 27, 1932, 80-82.

Guthrie, W. K. C.–*Orpheus and the Greeks,* Methuen, London, 1952.[2]
–*A History of Greek Philosophy,* Vol. 1: The Earlier Pre-Socratics and the Pythagoreans, Cambridge Univ. Press, 1962.
–*Plato's views on the nature of the Soul,* Recherches sur la tradition. Platonicienne in Entretiens sur l'antiquité classique, Toure, 3, Geneve, 1955, 3-19.

Hackforth, R.–*Plato's Phaedo,* trans. with introduction and commentary, Cambridge Univ. Press, 1955.
–*Plato's Theism,* Classical Quarterly, 30, 1936, 4-9.
–*Plato's Examination of Pleasure,* Cambridge Univ. Press, 1945.
–*Plato's Phaedrus,* trans. with introduction and commentary, Cambridge Univ. Press, 1952.
–*Plato's Cosmogony,* (Timaeus 27Dff), Classical Quarterly, N.S., 9, 1959, 17-22.
–*Plato's Phaedo,* trans. with introduction and commentary, Cambridge Univ. Press, 1955.
–*The Modification of Plan in Plato's Republic,* Classical Quarterly, 7, 1913, 265-272.

Hall, R. H.–*Plato and the Individual,* The Hague Nijhofl, 1963.

Hall, S. C.–*A Primer of Freudian Psychology,* 1954.

Hall, S. C. and G. Lindzey–*Theories of Personality,* N.Y., 1970.[2]

Hardie, W. F. R.–*A Study in Plato,* Oxford Univ. Press, 1936.

Harrison, J.—*Prolegomena to the Study of the Greek Religion*, N.Y., 1957.

Hebb, D. O.—*A Textbook of Psychology*, W. G. Saunders Co., Philadelphia, 1961.

Hendrick, I.—*Facts and Theories of Psychoanalysis, Laurel* edition, 1966.

Hoffmann, E.—*Die Griechische Philosophie bis Platon*, Heidelberg, 1951.

Howald, E.—*Eikos Logos*, Hermes, 57, 1922, 63-79.

Huonder, Q.—*Gott und Seele im lichte der Griechischen Philosophie*, Max Hueber, München, 1954.

Hutt, M. L., R. L. Isaacson and M. L. Blum—*Psychology*: the Science of Interpersonal Behavior, Harper & Row, N.Y.: 1965.

Ithurriagne, J.—*La Croyance de Platon: a l'Immortalite et a la Survie de l'Ame Humaine*, Libra Universitaire, J. Geunber, Paris, 1931.

Jaeger, W.—*Paedeia*, The Ideals of Greek Culture, trans. G. Highet, Vol. 2, B. Blackwell, Oxford, 1944.

Jean, F. C., E. C., Harrah and F. L. Herman—*Man and His Biological World*, revised edition, Ginn Co., N.Y. 1962.

Joseph, H. W. B.—*Plato's Republic: the comparison between the soul and the State, Essays in Ancient and Modern Philosophy* Oxford, 1935, 82-121.

Kenny, A. J. P.—*Mental Health in Plato's Republic*, Proceedings of British Academy IV, 1969, 238-41.

Kirk, G. S. and Raven, J. E.—*The Pre-Socratic Philosophers: a Critical History with a Selection of Texts*, Cambridge at the Univ. Press, 1957; paperback, 1962.

Klein, D. B.—*A History of Scientific Psychology*, Basic Books, Inc. N.Y./London, 1970.

Lee, H. D. P.—*Plato, the Republic*, trans. with an introduction, Penguin Books, 1964.

Lewis, J. and B. Towers—*Naked Ape or Homo Sapiens?*, N.Y., 1973.

Liddell, H. G. and R. Scott—*A Greek-English Lexikon*, Oxford, at the Clarendon Press, 1897.

Leon, P.—*The Homoioméries of the Anaxagoras,* Classical Quarterly, 21, 1927, 122-141.

Lodge, R. C.—*Mind in Platonism,* Philosophical Review, 35, 1926, 201-220.

—*Plato's Theory of Ethics,* Kegan Paul, London, 1928.

Loenen, J. H. M. M.—*De Nous in het Systeem Van Plato's Philosophie,* Dissertatie Universiteit van Amsterdam, Jasonpers Universiteistspers, Amsterdam, 1951.

Magalhaes-Vilhenade, V.—*La Probleme de Socrate,* Presse Univ. de France, Paris, 1952.

Marx, M. H. and W. A. Hillix—*Systems and Theories in Psychology,* McGraw-Hill Book Co., N.Y., 1963.

Missiak, H. and V. S. Sexton—*History of Psychology: An Overview,* Grune, Stratton, N.Y., 1966.

Monro, D. B.—*Homer, Iliad,* Books 1-24, Oxford at Clarendon Press, 1894.[5]

Moore, H. C.—*Pagan Ideas of Immortality during the Early Roman Empire,* Cambridge, 1918.

More, P. E.—*The Religion of Plato,* Princeton Univ. Press, 1921.

Morris, Desmond—*The Naked Ape,* London, 1967.

Mugnier, R.—*Le Sens du mot Theios chez Platon,* J. Vrin, Paris, 1930.

Mullahy, P.—*Oedipus: Myth and Complex: a Review of Psychoanalysis theory,* Grove Press, N.Y., 1957.

Muller, G.—*Studien zu den Platonischen Nomoi,* Ver C. H. Beck, Hunchen, 1951, in Zetemata, Monographien zur Klassischen Altertums—Wissenschaft, Heft 3.

Munroe, L. R.—*Schools of Psychoanalytic Thought,* The Dryden Press, 1956, N.Y.

Murphy, N. R.—*The Interpretation of Plato's Republic,* Oxford, at Clar. Press, 1960.

Murray, T. A.—*Homer, the Iliad,* with an introduction and English translation, London, 1937,[2] Vol. 1,[2] in Loeb Classical Library.

Nettleship, R. L.—*Lectures on the Republic of Plato,* MacMillan, London, 1898.

Nilsson, M. P.–*A History of Greek Religion, trans.* F. L. Fielden, Oxford, at the Clarendon Press, 1925.

Onians, R. B.–*The Origin of the European Thought,* Cambridge, 1951.

Owen, G. E. L.–*The Place of the Timaeus in Plato's Dialogues,* Classical Quarterly, N. S. 1953, 79-95.

Page, D.–*The Homeric Odyssey,* Oxford Univ. Press, 1955.

Plato–*Apology,* with introduction and English translation by H. N. Fowler, London, 1930, in the Loeb Classical Library.

Platt, R. B. and G. K. Reid–*Bioscience,* Reinhold Book Co., N.Y., 1967.

Plotini – Opera, tom 1, ed. by Henry et N. E. R. Schwyzer, Paris, 1951.

Popper, K. R.–*The Open Society and its Enemies,* Vol. 1, Plato, Routledge and Kegan Paul, London 1945; paperback, 1962.[4]

Pringle-Pattison, S. A.–*The Idea of Immortality,* Oxford, at Clarendon Press, 1922.

Rankin, H. D.–*Plato and the Individual,* Methuen, London, 1964.

Raven, J. E.–*The Basis of Anaxagoras' Cosmology,* Classical Quarterly, Vol. 4, 1954, 131-34.

Rees, D. A.–*Bipartition of the Soul in the Early Academy,* Journal of Hellenic Studies, (LXXVII) 77(1), 1957, 112-118.

Rich, A. N.–*The Platonic Ideas as the Thoughts of God,* Mnemosyne, S4, 7, 1954, 123-133.

Ritter, C.–*Platon,* 2, Beck, Munchen, 1910.

–*The Essence of Plato's Philosophy,* Allen and Unwin, London, 1933.

Robin, L.–*Greek Thought,* trans. M. R. Dobie, London, 1928.

–*Platon,* F. Alcom, Paris, 1935.

Rodier, G.–*Les preuves de l'immortalite d'apres le phedon,* Etudes de philosophie Grecque, J. Vrin, Paris, 1957, 138-154.

Rohde, E.–*Psyche: the cult of souls and belief among the Greeks* trans. by W. B. Hillis, Routledge & Kegan Paul Ltd., London, 1925.

Ross, Sir D.–*Plato's theory of Ideas,* Oxford Univ. Press, 1951.

Russell, B.—*A History of Western Philosophy and its connection with political and social circumstances from the earliest times to the present day,* G. Allen & Unwin Ltd., London, 1946; paperback, 1962.

Salmond, S. D. F.—*The Christian Doctrine of Immortality,* T. T. Clark, Edinburgh, 1895.

Sanders, T. J.—*Soul and State in Plato's Laws,* Eranos, (LX) 60, 1962, 37-55.

Sciacca, M. F.—*Il problema dell'immortalita dell'anima et metempsicosi in Platone, Studi Sula filosofia antica,* Napoli, 1935, p. 221.

Severin, F. T.—*Humanistic Viewpoints in Psychology: a book of readings,* McGraw-Hill Book Co., N.Y., 1965.

Shaerer, R.—*Dien l'homme et la vie d'apres Platon,* Neuchatel, 1944.

Shorey, P. *What Plato Said,* the Univ. Chicago Press, 1962.

—*The Idea of God in Plato's Republic,* Univ. of Chicago, Studies in Classical Philology, 1, 1895, 188-239.

—*Plato, the Republic: with an English translation and notes,* Vol. 1-2, N.Y., 1930 in L.C.L.

—*Unity of Plato's Thought,* Decennial Publications of the University of Chicago, (1st Ser.) 6, 120-214, Chicago, 1904.

—*The Timaeus of Plato,* American Journal of Philology, 10, 1889, 51-54.

—*Recent Interpretation of Timaeus,* Classical Philology, 23, 1928, 343-362.

Simson, W. E.—*Der Befriff der Seele bei Plato,* Leipzig, 1889.

Simpton, G. G.—*Biology and Man,* Harcourt, Brace and World Inc., N. Y., 1969.

Skemp, J. B.—*The Theory of Motion in Plato's Later Dialogues,* Cambridge, 1942.

—*Plato's Statesman,* a trans, with introductory essays and footnotes, Kegan Paul, London, 1952; paperback, 1961.

Skinner, B. F.—*The Behavior of Organism: an experimental analysis,* N.Y., Appleton-Century-Crofts, 1938.

—*Science and Human Behavior,* N.Y., MacMillan, 1953.

—*Beyond Freedom and Dignity*, paperback, Bantam-Vintage Bks., N.Y., 1972.

—*Walden Two, paperback,* MacMillan, 1972.

Snell, B.—*The Discovery of the Mind: the Greek Origins of European Thought,* Blackwell, Oxford, 1953.

Solmsen, F.—*Plato's Theology,* Ithaca, N.Y., 1942.

Stein, J.—*Effective Personality: a humanistic approach*, Brooks/Cole Publ. Co., Belmont, Ca., 1972.

Stewart, J. A.—*Plato's Doctrine of Ideas,* Oxford Univ. Press, 1909.

Stock, J. L.—*Plato and the Tripartite of the Soul,* Mind, 2A, 1915, 207-221.

Strupp, H. H.—*An Introduction to Freud and Modern Psychoanalysis,* Barrow's Educational Series, N.Y., 1967.

Taylor, A. E.—*Plato: The Man and his Work,* Methuen, London, 1960; paperback, 1960.

—*A Commentary on Plato's Timaeus,* Oxford at the Clarendon Press, 1962.

—*Plato, The Laws,* trans. with an introduction, in Everyman's Library, London, 1960.

—*Plato's theology,* Mind, LII, (52), 1943, 178-182.

—*The Mind of Plato* (originally Plato, published by Constable Ltd., 1922), Ann Arbor paperbacks, the Univ. of Michigan Press, 1960.

Temple, W.—*Plato and Christianity,* London, 1916.

Thompson, C.—*Psychoanalysis: Evolution and Development,* Grove Press, N.Y., 1957.

Vlastos, G.—*The Disorderly Motion,* Classical Quarterly, 33, 1939, 71-83.

—*On Heraclitus,* American Journal of Philology, 76, 1955, 337-368.

—*The Physical Theory of Anaxagoras,* Philosophical Review, Vol. 59, 1950, 31-57.

Watson, R. I.—*The Great Psychologists: From Aristotle to Freud,* J. B. Lippincott Co., N. Y., 1963.

—*Psychology as a Behaviorist Views It*, Psych. Rev., 20, 1913, 112, 158-77.

—*Behavior: An Introduction to Comparative Psychology*, N. Y., Holt, Rinehart, Winston, Inc., 1914.

—*Behaviorism, rev. ed., University of Chicago Press*, Chicago, 1966.

White, A. R.—*The Philosophy of Mind*, Random House, N.Y., 1968.

Wiggins, J. S., K. S. Renner, G. L. Clore and R. J. Rose—*The Psychology of Personality*, Addison-Wesley Publ. Co., Reading, Mass., 1971.

Wilamowitz-Moellendroff, U. V.—*Platon*, Vol. 1-2, Berlin, 1919.

Wolman, B. B.—*Contemporary Theories and Systems in Psychology*, Harper and Row, Publ., N.Y., 1963.

—*The Unconscious Mind: The Meaning of Freudian Psychology*, Prentice-Hall, N. J. (paperback), 1968.

Woodsworth, R. S. and M. R. Sheenan—*Contemporary Schools and Psychology*, the Ronald Press, Co., N.Y., 1964.[3]

Xenophon—*Cyropaedia*, with an English translation and introduction by W. Miller, London, 1914 Vol. 2, in the Loeb Classical Library.

—*Memorabilia and Oeconomicus*, with an introduction and English translation by E. C. Marchant, London, 1923, in the Loeb Classical Library.

Zeller, E.—*Pre-Socratic Philosophy: A History of Greek Philosophy from the Earliest Period to the time of Socrates*, trans. S. F. Alleyne, Vol. 1-2, Longmans, London, 1881.

—*Socrates and the Socratic School*, trans. O. J. Reichel, Longmans, London, 1877.[2]

—*Plato and the Older Academy*, trans. S. F. Alleyne, Russell, N.Y. (1888), 1962.

Zilboorg, G.—*Sigmund Freud, His Exploration of the Mind of Man*, N.Y., Norton, 1941.

INDEX